UNRECONCILED

UNRECONCILED

FAMILY, TRUTH, AND INDIGENOUS RESISTANCE

JESSE WENTE

ALLEN
LANE

ALLEN LANE

an imprint of Penguin Canada, a division of Penguin Random House Canada Limited

Canada • USA • UK • Ireland • Australia • New Zealand • India • South Africa • China

First published 2021

www.penguinrandomhouse.ca

LIBRARY AND ARCHIVES CANADA CATALOGUING IN PUBLICATION

Title: Unreconciled : family, truth, and Indigenous resistance / Jesse Wente.
Names: Wente, Jesse, author.
Identifiers: Canadiana (print) 20200405284 | Canadiana (ebook) 20200405365 |
ISBN 9780735235731 (hardcover) | ISBN 9780735235748 (EPUB)
Subjects: LCSH: Wente, Jesse. | LCSH: Indigenous men—Canada—Identity. | LCSH:
Indigenous peoples—Canada—Biography. | LCSH: Indigenous peoples—Canada—
Social conditions. | LCSH: Reconciliation. | LCSH: Canada—Ethnic relations. |
LCSH: Canada—Race relations. | LCGFT: Autobiographies.
Classification: LCC E99.C6 W46 2021 | DDC 305.897/333071092—dc23

Book design by Matthew Flute
Cover design by Matthew Flute
Cover images: (TV) © Steven Errico, (man) © OlegEvseev,
(frames) © Mykhailo Polenok / EyeEm, all Getty Images

Manufactured in Canada

10 9 8 7 6 5 4 3 2 1

For Norma and Barbara

Prologue

I remember the exact moment I learned I was an Indian.

It was a summer afternoon when I was about ten. My softball team was playing in Topham Park, just around the corner from our home in Toronto's East York, and I was coming up to bat, crossing the infield dirt to take my place at the plate.

Wah-wah-wah-wah-wah-wah-wah.

The league was a local one, both teams made up of kids from the neighbourhood. I'd played in it from the time I was five, starting out in T-ball on the smallest of Topham's three diamonds and working up to the big field, which had dugouts, a scoreboard with an announcer's booth, grandstands, and makeshift bullpens where the pitchers could warm up. I'd walk over to watch when the men's teams played there at night, the big lights turning everything a bright, washed-out yellow. The ball would almost glow when hit into the air, and, if it carried far enough, would fade into the darkness as it sailed beyond the reach of the light poles.

Baseball was big for our family then. My dad, who'd grown up a Cubs fan in Chicago, had embraced the Blue Jays when the franchise was born in 1977. He'd listen to games on a transistor radio he carried while doing work around the house, or watch them with me on the little Zenith TV in the living room. Occasionally he'd buy the cheap outfield tickets you could get at the grocery store during the summer, and we'd see a game at Exhibition Stadium in seats that were angled a little bit off so that you had to turn slightly to take in the action. Dad played third base and some outfield in a slo-pitch league for a while, too, and would later coach both me and my sister. Some of my fondest childhood memories are of spending time with him at the batting cage or playing catch at the park.

In our softball games it was common for players to make cracks at the opposition, refrains that tended to max out at the "We want a pitcher, not a belly itcher" level. That bruising psychological warfare was mostly directed at the better players because, hey, they were good. I would classify myself as just okay all around but bordering on good at the plate; I'd make consistent contact and was patient enough to take a walk if the pitcher couldn't find the zone, which happened regularly. And when I did catch hold of one I could hit it far, a combination of decent technique and being fairly big for my age. So getting jeered at wasn't unusual, and was maybe even expected. It was something you laughed off or ignored, just a part of the game.

What I heard that particular afternoon was something different, though. Not one of the rhymes or cracks, repeated to the point where they lost all meaning, that rang out when other kids went up to bat. This was a sound reserved for me.

Wah-wah-wah-wah-wah-wah-wah.

It started all at once, as if they'd met up to plan it before the game, all the opposing players flapping their hands in front of their open mouths

2

to make the noise: "Wah-wah-wah-wah-wah-wah-wah." They were war whooping.

It was a sound I'd heard before, but I couldn't place it immediately, or maybe I didn't want to. Later, when I was old enough to get stopped by the police, I'd become more familiar with that pattern of thought: pushing aside the certain knowledge of why this was happening to look for some *good* reason, some reason other than the fact that my identity alone could incite in another person a desire to do harm. That my simple existence could be seen as a provocation or offence.

I knew the noise, though; I knew what it meant, and that understanding could be delayed for only so long. I knew it from Saturday morning cartoons, watched from behind a bowl of cereal, the last of the milk disappearing to reveal the sugar clumped at the bottom. It was the noise made by the Indians Bugs Bunny killed, counting them off on a chalkboard and singing as he went: "One little, two little, three little Injuns. Four little, five little, six little Injuns—oops sorry, that one was a half-breed," scrubbing a mark in half as he corrected himself. It was made in the movies I watched on TV by the savages that besieged the good settlers on their journey of destiny, the savages who had to be vanquished to set the world right.

The kids on the other team knew what it meant, too. They'd seen the same cartoons and the same kind of movies. Their parents, who would have known my parents, also understood. As did the coaches, though no adult stepped in to put a stop to it. It meant I was an Indian. The bad guy. The savage. The loser.

Now, it certainly wouldn't have been news to me to be identified as Anishinaabe or Ojibwe. I had known myself as both for as long I could remember, not unlike the way I knew that my dad was American. My family didn't drape itself in our ethnic background, but it wasn't hidden. It was just what we were. It's why we occasionally ate frybread and corn soup. Why sometimes we drove for hours to visit our family in Serpent River. Why I had a middle name that no one else did. That's what being

Ojibwe was to me at the time, a collection of unremarkable and ever-present givens. I had never known anything else.

But I'd never thought of myself as an Indian in the way it suddenly seemed everyone else did. Nor had I imagined that my Indianness made me significantly different from any other kid in the neighbourhood. It did, though, and those kids wanted me to know it. They wanted me to feel what it was like to be reduced to a caricature in less time than it took me to step to the plate. To feel what it was like to have my interests and passions, my love of baseball and movies, my family's history and my hopes for the future stripped away and replaced with a sound I'd never made, a sound I'd never heard *any* First Nations person make—except on a screen.

I'd love to say that the whole thing ended with me crushing a ball beyond the left-fielder's head, but I can't even remember what happened next. It's only the whooping that has stayed with me.

Sadly, it has stayed with Canada, too. In late May 2018 a news story about an AAA youth hockey tournament in Quebec City caught my attention. After a bantam team called the First Nations Elites, made up of thirteen- and fourteen-year-old boys from several nations in Quebec, Ontario, and Nova Scotia, won the opening game of the Coupe Challenge Quebec AAA, the opposing players raised their hands in unison and made the same sound.

Wah-wah-wah-wah-wah-wah-wah.

This was just one of several racist incidents the Elites would be subjected to over the course of the competition. They would face unfair treatment from tournament referees, taunts from spectators that included calling them "savages," and, according to Christina Gull, the mother of a boy on the team, the playing of powwow music by the arena DJ.

"I was thinking, 'Does this still exist?'" Gull said to the CBC shortly after the tournament. "'Are we in the eighties or nineties?'"

4

At the time of that softball game in Topham Park, residential schools were still open. If I'd lived in a more remote community I could have been in one. And when the Elites took the ice in that youth hockey tournament, the final report of the Truth and Reconciliation Commission was already nearly three years old. Still, despite taking place more than thirty years apart, the two incidents shared intention, effect, and origin. They were intended to demean, distract, and dehumanize. They hurt and they lingered. I still vividly remember that sound, and I suspect that the boys of the First Nations Elites, and everyone else who's ever heard that sound on the field of play, remember it too. It's always there, a reminder of who is us and who is them.

That lack of progress across three and a half decades should be shocking, something Gull highlighted in the thoughts she shared with the CBC. To many First Nations people, though, the shock at a racist act can last only so long and run only so deep, even if the pain lingers. We simply face this shit too often to be surprised by it—a world-weariness we surely share with other marginalized communities. And, really, we know better than to expect these attacks to stop when so many of their underlying causes remain unchanged and barely addressed.

To be clear, before the other kids made that whooping sound at that softball game, I'd never heard it outside of movies or cartoons. Since then I've been around the world and visited many Indigenous nations, and I've still never heard it anywhere else. There are, of course, nations who whoop. But they sound nothing like the movies, and certainly nothing like what I heard on the diamond that day. The sound those kids made is an invention of Hollywood.

In fact, most non-Indigenous people's entire understanding of Indigenous life and personhood is an invention of Hollywood, from the war whoop to the sense that colonialism is inevitable, that the land and its original inhabitants are simply impediments to the birthright of the newcomers, that we are objects to be either used or destroyed on a white man's path to destiny. This has been the dominant portrait of Indigenous life at least as far back as the birth of moving pictures. Our expendability on screen is so written into Hollywood that it was common for many years for a group of extras to be called "a bunch of Indians" by those on set. A group of *Star Wars* stormtroopers waiting in the wings is a bunch of Indians.

The kids who whooped at me that day were weaponizing one of the only things they knew about First Nations people. That it was entirely a fiction speaks to the incredible power of media representation, of storytelling. That it could hurt me so deeply despite being a lie also speaks to that power. And the fact that the same sound is still employed to mock First Nations kids decades later indicates that little has changed around the inclusion of Indigenous peoples in media and education. This is still a sound that represents much of what people think they know about us, even if the cartoons don't play on Saturday mornings anymore and Hollywood now seldom makes westerns.

The misrepresentation is a purposeful one. Its aim is to undermine the value of Indigenous lives and the value of Indigenous claims to the land stolen from us, and its consequences stretch far beyond taunts and jeers. It is the narrative used to justify genocide and its tools: residential schools, forced separation of families, violation of treaty rights, indifference to the lives of missing and murdered Indigenous women, lack of access to education and safe water. Storytelling is one of the key methods used by colonizers to explain and obscure their lawless treatment of the lands and peoples over which they claim dominion.

But storytelling is also one of our best weapons in the fight to reclaim our rightful place.

For much of my professional career I've worked toward making space for Indigenous storytellers. As a film critic and festival programmer, I strove to bring attention to the work of Indigenous creators. As a radio columnist, I continue to highlight major issues facing the First Nations community, and to act as a medium for larger messages when I can. As founding director of the Indigenous Screen Office, I work to build a new ecosystem for Indigenous filmmakers that may one day allow them to realize visions as big as any of those of Lucas, Cameron, Spielberg, or Scorsese.

I champion these artists' work for the same reasons any great art is celebrated—because it is beautiful, honest, brave, and any number of other wonderful and affecting things. But I've dedicated my life to it because of my unwavering belief in the power of Indigenous representation to improve the quality of Indigenous life and make Canada, as a whole, a better place.

Colonial systems have always pushed assimilation and exploitation as the only way to survive and succeed, the only way forward. My own family made great efforts and greater sacrifices as we were forced into that narrative. If we gave up our land and culture, our communities and identities, we could become Canadian, the story went. But the myth of that path to progress was so flimsy that it could be exposed by a group of ten-year-old softball players. Even when racialized people do exactly what Canada demands of them, their Canadianness and the protections it supposedly affords can be stripped away in a moment. No matter what they tell you, you can still be reduced to your most obvious physical traits.

Progress built on a lie is not progress. A lie cannot improve this country or the lives of the people in it. But I still wonder how the truth could have changed things that afternoon in Topham Park. Would those kids have whooped that way if they'd known that no real Indian ever did? Would their parents have stopped them if they themselves hadn't been conditioned to think of First Nations people as worthy of scorn and erasure? Would anyone have singled out that aspect of my identity at all if they'd seen real representations of Indigenous life?

I can't say for sure. But I have conviction about the ways truth can change Canada. If we ever hope to see a functional relationship between this country and its First Nations people, it has to grow from honesty and understanding—the basis cannot be a lie. Laying that foundation will require Canada to face up to what it is, what it has always been. It will require this country to listen to the stories that Indigenous people have been telling for more than a hundred and fifty years. It will require truth.

This book is my truth.

PART I

The Stories I Was Told

CHAPTER 1

Nookomis in the Kitchen

I always loved spending time with my grandmother Norma, particularly while she cooked. Our house on Westview Boulevard had a yellow kitchen with a brown linoleum table tucked into a booth as if it had been relocated from a diner. I'd sit at that table surrounded by those warm colours and talk to her or draw or do my homework while she moved around the room, her hands gliding with quiet assurance in and out of mixing bowls and bags of flour, her face haloed by her dark curly hair. She was a small woman, but for me at least her presence was large and comforting. And the food she made for us was a manifestation of that comfort—pies and roasts and mashed potatoes.

We'd moved to East York, a small Toronto suburb, on the eve of my second birthday in April 1976, chiefly to be closer to Norma and my grandfather Jack. Our bungalow stood on a corner lot with a beautiful white-and-pink-blooming magnolia tree out front and two massive maples, one in the backyard and the other at the side of the house. The back patio was shaded by a vine that in the summer produced huge purple grapes. My mom would make jam from them, letting my sister,

Maggie, and me pick what was left and sell it from a makeshift farm stand at the end of the driveway. Norma and Jack lived across the street in a house with a long driveway and a well-tended vegetable garden.

My parents, Jim and Connie, met in high school at Malvern Collegiate while circulating in the same group of friends—a bohemian mix of artists and ne'er-do-wells—and got together shortly after graduation. They were young when I was born, my mom twenty and my dad twenty-one, a pair of hippies living in a rented house on Waverley Road. My dad had a job making sails at the time, and my mother looked after me. She also watched my cousin Sean, who was like a brother, while her sister Bonnie was at work, taking us both out in a stroller to walk along the beach. Maggie came along when I was eighteen months old.

The move to East York was a big one for my family. My dad's mom, Barbara, and stepfather, Thomas, who were both executives and well off, helped my parents with the down payment, meaning this was a house all our own, not a rental. There was an in-law suite in the basement that Bonnie and Sean moved into, but most of the rest of the house was original and had been well maintained. It still had a functioning milk box built into the wall by the side door, where the milkman had once dropped off his bottles.

Both of my parents eventually got jobs in a nearby industrial park that also housed an enormous Peek Freans factory; when the wind blew in the right direction, the whole neighbourhood would be filled with the smell of cookies. My mom started as a clerk at Con Chem Ltd., which makes all manner of toothpastes and hair products. My dad was a purchasing agent at Scepter/Ipex, a manufacturer of plastic piping. Both would stay with the same company for more than three decades and retire as executives—a form of upward mobility practically unheard of today.

When my mom returned to work, it was Norma who stepped in to care for me, Maggie, and Sean. Later, after my grandfather Jack passed away, she moved in with us full time. Eleven-year-old me was thrilled to have her around more, but it was only as an adult that I fully realized what an incredible gift her presence was.

Norma Meawasige was born in 1927 on what is now called the Serpent River First Nation, a reserve a couple hours' drive west of Sudbury, just down the hill from Elliot Lake, Ontario. Her father, Alex, had been chief there, and her mother, Maggie, originally from the nearby Sagamok First Nation, was the community's medicine woman and midwife. Alex and Maggie had a family farm and were particularly known for their potatoes. When they harvested their lettuces, corn, berries, or any other crop they'd keep only a portion for themselves and their eight children. The rest they would share with the community.

My great-grandparents spoke mostly Ojibwe, but they believed that a certain degree of assimilation—including having their kids master English—would be a pathway to a brighter future. This was, I've learned from conversations with my cousin Marilyn, less an endorsement of the opportunities Canada provided than a prescient acknowledgment of what form that future would inevitably take. Their farm was right next to the reserve, but off it; in Alex's view, the government-designated reserves were dead-end places. He knew his children would never be able to live the kind of life he had. Change was coming whether he liked it or not, and he and Maggie wanted their children to be as pre-pared for it as possible.

They were devout Catholics—having been won over by the mission-aries who'd settled the church twenty kilometres away in the town of Spanish—and they had achieved no small measure of success trading furs to the Hudson's Bay Company. It was a classic story.

My great-grandfather ran his trapline right up until the 1970s, when the forest was clear-cut. He died shortly after my family moved into the East York house, and Maggie passed about a year later, but even though I didn't get a lot of time with them, they did leave me something immensely valuable: my sacred name.

As the story goes, before I was born, my great-grandparents had a dream about me. In the dream, a small baby is blown into the community by the north wind, tumbling in the air before landing in the centre of the river from which the reserve draws its name. They took the dream as a warning, and told my mother that she had to call me Nodin— meaning wind—or I would be stillborn. My parents used Nodin as one of my middle names. I'm the only one in the family with a name like this. It's an odd distinction, but one I've always cherished and tried to live up to.

Alex and Maggie were people with strong physical and spiritual connections to the land and the community, but they also recognized that there was a predominant Canadian culture, and they wanted their kids to be prepared for it. Education was, to them, a gateway to opportunities not available on the reserve, so they very well may have chosen to send their kids to residential school in Spanish—if they'd had a choice. In the Canada of the early 1930s, though, they didn't: First Nations, Métis, and Inuit children were required by law to attend. Six of Alex and Maggie's eight children went to the Spanish Indian Residential Schools, St. Peter Claver School for Boys and St. Joseph's School for Girls; only the youngest escaped. Their family, including my *nookomis*, Norma, would learn that the reality of a colonial education was nothing like the promise.

I was eleven the first and only time my grandmother spoke to me about what she endured at residential school. She'd moved in with us just that year, and we were in the kitchen together. I asked her why our family didn't speak Ojibwe, why I heard only small snatches of it when we visited Serpent River and the elders played cards. She stopped what she was doing and looked at me for a long moment, maybe assessing whether I was ready for the answer, and then began to tell me matter-of-factly what the nuns at St. Joseph's did to her whenever she was caught speaking her language. She told me how they'd make her stick out her tongue and then hit it with a ruler. She told me that they'd also beat her for any-thing else they perceived as a failure or disobedience, sometimes hitting her with a shoe. Even in recounting this, she didn't really speak badly of the school, instead saying that being taught English had served her well.

Whether she was spared other abuses or simply chose to shelter me from the knowledge of them, I don't know. Survivors of the schools in Spanish have described unimaginable acts of physical, emotional, and sexual abuse, some of which occurred during the same period of time she was there. They have also described the efforts designed to erase them: nutritionless meals that pushed them to the edge of starvation; nuns who referred to them by assigned numbers instead of their names.

My grandmother was allowed back home with her parents only for the summers and occasional holidays. Almost all of the childhood photos I have of her are from these too-short stretches, smiling and playing with her siblings, though I also have two school photos in which she appears deeply sad. In them, she and her classmates stand in sackcloth dresses with their hair shorn, cut forcibly by the Daughters of the Heart of Mary, the Roman Catholic order that administered the school. Norma spent ten years of her life at St. Joseph's, from the age of six until she was sixteen.

By the time she graduated, the desire to speak Ojibwe had been beaten out of her and Serpent River no longer felt like home. The curriculum at St. Joseph's had been aimed at training Indigenous girls to work as domestics and cleaners in white households and busi-nesses, the only careers to which the architects of that racist school system felt First Nations, Métis, and Inuit girls should aspire. When Norma moved to Toronto shortly after the Second World War, that's exactly what she became. Though she stayed in touch with her family and continued to visit Serpent River, she stopped identifying herself as an Indigenous woman anywhere else; when she had to, she claimed to be Italian. It made life a little bit easier, sparing her from ridicule and the very real possibility of state interference.

In Toronto she met my grandfather, Jack Feltham, a white veteran just back from the war. Jack was twenty years her senior and had badly damaged his back while fighting in Europe, an injury that would trouble him for the rest of his life. He drove a truck and worked other odd jobs, but by the time I was born his back problems had put an end to his working days. I knew him as a larger-than-life personality who was very generous with his grandkids.

Jack and Norma settled in a ramshackle house in the Beaches and had three kids: my mom, Aunt Bonnie, and Uncle Rob. My grandmother eventually moved from domestic work to a job as a hostess at the Albany Club in the city's downtown core. The oldest private club in Canada, the Albany was founded by John A. Macdonald and caters to wealthy conservatives. She would work there for the better part of three decades, until her retirement. Separated from her family, her language, our stories, and our land, living with a white man, and spending her days waiting on colonial elites, my grandmother was in many ways a victory for residential schools. She was the exact type of Indian they had hoped to produce.

Apart from the occupants themselves, very little in our East York house would have identified us as Indigenous: some foods my classmates would've labelled "weird" or "different," some framed pictures from Serpent River, and a series of paintings of chiefs that belonged to my grandmother. That's about it. There were no ceremonies, no obvious ties to any cultural tradition. My grandmother didn't do that stuff. Unlike her parents, she never spoke Ojibwe in her home. My mom and her siblings were raised without the language, as were my sister and I.

We didn't interact with any other Indigenous people in the city, either. It's not that there weren't any, though certainly the number in East York was low; it's just that we didn't cross paths with them. The opportunities didn't really exist. There were no downtown powwows, no gathering places or First Nations schools, no cultural centres. Until

I went to university, the only Indians I knew were related to me. Even when we'd go to the rez, everyone we spent time with was a relative of some kind.

We were alone, distant from the land and tradition, having more in common with our neighbours than our ancestors. Like my grandmother, then, my sister and I, Sean, my mother, my aunt and uncle—we were all the exact type of Indians residential schools were designed to produce.

It's painful to grapple with the knowledge that St. Joseph's and the racist system that conceived it are foundational to who I am as a person—where I was born, how I was raised, the man I've become. If it wasn't for that horrible place, everything it took from my grandmother and everything it inflicted on her, who knows how her life might have turned out? It's hard to imagine her ending up in Toronto without first being so violently severed from her family and community. If she hadn't moved to the city and raised her kids there, my mom and dad would likely never have met.

Of course, the same if/then revisionism is possible on my dad's side—just as it's possible for pretty much anyone to do—but in that family history, the choices, even the painful ones, are freely made because the people doing the choosing are white. My grandmother was not afforded that agency. Her pain and loss weren't the result of a misstep or a bad decision; they were part of a state-sponsored policy of physical and cultural eradication. And that policy didn't officially end until Saskatchewan's Gordon's Indian Residential School closed its doors in 1996, just two years before my grandmother's death. Even now, the policy is still pursued unofficially.

I think of Norma every day. I think of how fortunate I am to have spent the time I did with her, to have been told her story when so many of the elders, storytellers, and knowledge keepers who could have truly illuminated the past are now available only as spirits. I feel an enormous obligation to do right by her, an obligation I believe the rest of this country should feel as well. And I know at a deep level that everything she lost, everything my family lost, can never be replaced.

I am trying to live a life that honours hers. She is owed that and so much more.

CHAPTER 2

Big City and Small Country

The thought nags at me now, but as a kid I never wondered what I was missing out on growing up away from Serpent River. A few times a year we'd pile into the car and drive to the north shore of Lake Huron. The trip took about five hours, not a quick jaunt by any measure, but as I sat in the back seat and gazed out the window, time would stretch and it would become a journey of epic proportions—Frodo and company's *Lord of the Rings* walk recreated in a family sedan. Getting out of the car when we finally arrived felt like stepping into another world.

The main differences were obvious: Toronto was the big city and Serpent River was the small country. There were moose around; the adults often carried rifles in case the opportunity to bag dinner presented itself. As a city kid who was never around guns, the sight of any of my aunties casually walking with a rifle seemed a bit odd. And there was much less to do on the rez, at least by my city standards. No theatres or restaurants or pro sports, just a ballpark, a hall, and the graveyard. The smoke shop that greeted you as you turned off the highway was the only store. If you wanted "civilization" you had to drive to Spanish, which barely qualified, or up the hill to Elliot Lake or Cutler, which was closer and had one diner and a corner store. There's a community centre and a big gym on the rez now, but I imagine my cousins were pretty starved for things to do at times as they got older. For me, though, that was never much of a problem over the few days our visits would last.

Other differences, big and small, mattered more. For instance, I was always aware that more people looked like me in Serpent River than in any other place I'd ever been. My cousins and I all bear a strong resemblance, and it sometimes seemed as if everyone was a cousin, aunt, uncle, or some other relation. They weren't, not all of them, at least; Serpent River is small, but not that small. Still, with fewer than four hundred people on the rez, everyone knew everyone, and if I came across a Meawasige we'd be able to find a link somewhere on the big genealogy chart that hung in the smoke shop, mapping family lines back as far as they were knowable. In Serpent River people didn't call me Jesse, they called me Nodin, the Anishinaabe name my great-grandparents gave me. There was a welcome, and welcoming, familiarity to that, part of the warmth and understanding that radiated in many ways through the entirety of our visits. Being in Serpent River brought a unique sense of family and community—it gave me something bigger to be a part of in a way no other place ever truly has. That I experienced this only during occasional visits, rather than daily life, is one of the losses I feel so acutely today.

It wasn't simply the fact of being around more of my family, either, because I never felt the same way when we visited my dad's family in Chicago. I loved the big American city, and have fond memories of Wilmette Harbor, where my grandfather Bill was harbour master. But it felt more like Toronto than Serpent River ever has.

There were a few key highlights of any trip up north. The biggest was swimming in the river. The community lies just off the highway, and at a particular spot you could pull your car off the road and jump in—the current wasn't very strong and it was deep enough that you could safely high-dive off the rocks. The water was always very cold, but you acclimatized after the first freezing plunge. Everybody swam there, and still does. It was a place where you could spend hours on a hot summer day and see a good portion of the community, particularly the kids.

We'd also hike up to what was called Clear Lake. It seems to me that every place has a "Clear Lake," but the name was apt. There was no road in through the forest, and when I was a kid there'd never been a motorboat on the lake. You could dip a cup in and drink the water. In subsequent years, a road was built and the boats came. Now, you don't drink the water.

A dozen of us would make the trek: eight or so kids, some parents—carrying a canoe to leave for the season if it was spring—and an auntie with a gun. Partway there you'd cross some old train tracks, overgrown with trees hanging close on both sides, possibly the original line that had been run through the area. For me, that was the major landmark. There was a beach at the lake; we'd set up there and have a picnic, swim, and canoe. Only when it started to get dark would we trundle back, trying not to get eaten by the bugs.

Hunting has always been a big part of my family's life but it has never been a part of mine. I remember my cousin Junior preparing to go hunting, but I didn't go with him. I was always a little intimidated by the men's stories. Junior told me that to bring down a moose you had to shoot it in the eye—hitting the brain and killing it instantly—or else it would get pissed off and come chase you. That was bullshit to scare a little kid, but it's certainly true that you want to kill a moose on the first go if possible . . . so it doesn't get pissed off and come chase you. They are big, dangerous animals.

On my most recent trip north, Junior explained his actual technique, which is to try to shoot the animal through the throat and then track it until it falls, usually no more than a hundred feet from where it's hit. That version doesn't lack drama, in my opinion, but Junior's stories, like all good hunting and fishing stories, are always ratcheted up a notch, ridiculous but immensely entertaining. To hear him describe it these days, as soon as the moose hear his truck approach they throw in the towel and just walk out of the woods to die.

The good hunting ground was, perhaps unsurprisingly, not on the rez but ten or fifteen kilometres up the highway. The best fishing and farmland was likewise located nearby rather than on reserve territory. There's a story, repeated often in my family, about the year my great-grandfather went out to lay his trapline only to find that the forest that made up our ancient hunting grounds had been completely clear-cut— levelled in a matter of days or weeks with no notice given to the community. Lore has it that our family had hunted there as long as there'd been a family to go hunting, but since the forest was off the reserve, my great-grandfather had no say in what was done to it, even as chief. When he saw it, he sat down and wept.

Where the community is located now is a creation of the state. We'd once lived across a large territory that spanned the area north of Lake Huron. We were not concentrated into a small, hardscrabble space the way we are now. The land set aside for the reserve is the land colonial powers could see no easy way to exploit. When Anishinaabe communities signed the Robinson-Huron Treaty in 1850, they were left with the land the Crown was willing to relinquish. In the settlers' eyes, the fact that we were still permitted to hunt and fish in the places where we'd always hunted and fished would have been seen as a concession.

That story is sadly repeated in the histories of First Nations across this country, and the way it usually unfolds is the way it unfolded for Serpent River: The treaty was signed but only truly honoured by one side. The colonizers took all the land, more than they were allocated under the treaty. They implemented a system of government for our community that we never agreed to and then transferred the treaty from the Crown to this new state of Canada, even though we never agreed to that either. Then corporations clear-cut the forest, mined everything they could extract from the ground, poisoned the river, and left only when they could find nothing else to take.

Farther north, the RCMP and Quebec Provincial Police began to implement a policy in the 1950s that was designed to force the Inuit off their land and into settlements. Exploiting a loophole in an agricultural law, they started culling Inuit communities' sled dogs, dogs that were crucial to the Inuit way of life. Like the rez, the settlement itself is a colonial invention, because that's not how the Inuit lived. They lived out in open space, not settling in one spot but moving across the land by dogsled. So the colonizers took the dogs.

It was a process designed to grind a community to dust. And the fact that it didn't succeed—the fact that we persist in the far north, in Serpent River, in Canada—speaks to the amazing ability of Indigenous people to create and maintain rich, tight-knit communities. Even when we're cornered we make the community wherever we are. It is a beautiful trait and, for me as a kid visiting Serpent River, there was no clearer expression of that closeness and the joy it brings than our family feasts.

Our visits were always organized around feasts. Either we made the trip because one was planned or one was planned because we made the trip. The Meawasiges were and are one of the four or five big families in Serpent River, so the meal could easily draw a crowd of twenty or thirty or more.

There would be a single long table, piled with food, and a fire burning. There was a strict order to who could eat when—elders and children ate first, adult men last—but before any of the living had a bite, the spirits had to be offered their share. Each person would take a small piece of everything and bring it to the fire—apart from those pieces, you weren't allowed to touch the food. You would throw your sacrifice into the fire, giving your thanks and an acknowledgment to the ancestors as it burned. After that, you could eat.

The rez looked like a sparse suburb, with postwar bungalows and simple two-storey houses surrounded by pockets of undeveloped land.

Most of my closest family lived in one of those residential areas, their houses close together on either side of the street, allowing the cousins to run from one to the next. Our feasts would usually be laid out in their sizable shared yard.

The spread was country food: vegetables and meat the adults would have harvested or hunted themselves, and fresh-caught fish. Very little was store-bought, aside from beer and maybe some chips. I remember eating moose sloppy joes, which was a kind attempt to disguise the unfamiliar meat and make it more palatable to the city kids. (Moose is delicious, for the record.) Despite the nods to pickiness, though, the eating was truly nose-to-tail, often literally. Beaver tail made an occasional appearance—not the carnival confection you're likely thinking of, but rather a chewy and sort of gristly piece of meat. And on one particularly memorable occasion, the big event was when a moose nose was brought out.

It was huge, carried in on a large serving tray that it completely filled. I remember that the elders got really excited, including my grandmother. They gathered around the tray, each holding a spoon. The nose had been cooked to a gelatinous consistency. All those partaking dug in as if they were sharing a big bowl of ice cream, dipping in and raising big soft spoonfuls of nose. I remember someone telling me it was a delicacy, but I didn't believe them. It was the most disgusting thing I'd ever seen.

Moments of genuine culture shock like that were rare for me, in part because Serpent River wasn't a particularly traditional place. Colonialism moved across Canada from east to west, and eastern Indigenous communities were and are affected by it differently from western communities. First Nations in the east have been under colonial governance longer, so many of their traditions have disappeared more completely than in the west. My grandmother's forced separation from her community and whatever parts of traditional life she'd known was an experience shared by many people of her generation. Having had language and tradition beaten out of them in residential schools, they raised their own children without those things. At the same time, harsh economic realities on the rez drove more and more of us off it in search of jobs and other opportunities. For the last thirty years or so, though, there have been concerted efforts to reconnect with our traditions and identity. Community members brought back the powwow in the early nineties and have more recently begun offering Ojibwe language classes. But my childhood visits occurred before that resurgence. When my family went back to Serpent River for feasts, the pull for those who'd moved away wasn't tradition so much as the elders themselves—my great-grandparents and their contemporaries and later my grandmother and hers—the individuals who bound us, and brought us together in celebration.

By the time my sister and I were in high school my parents had both risen through the ranks of their respective companies, and with all of us leading independent lives, it was harder to get our schedules to align. We visited Serpent River less frequently. And when we did go, I felt a gulf between me and my cousins that I'd never noticed as a kid. We were all teenagers, everyone was a little bit more fully formed, and there was definitely more awareness of the fact that I wasn't part of the rez in the same way they were.

I don't know when exactly I started to feel that gulf between my cousins' experience and my own as a loss—as something I'd missed out on. It did happen, though; I feel that way now. And I think that change has a lot more to do with the evolution of the way I see myself than it does with any shift in how I see Serpent River.

There's no denying that Serpent River is an economically depressed place. By the time I was introduced to it, colonialism had already run its full course. Settlers had taken all they could take. And as those extractive natural resource industries left with their pockets bulging, they took what little opportunities had been allowed people on the rez. Youth in particular had little to aspire to, at least not without moving elsewhere. So young people tended to leave. That is a purposeful outcome.

It's an intentional erosion of the community, designed to diminish the number of rights holders so that, eventually, the country can point to the lack of people on the reserve as an excuse to ignore treaty terms. It's as if politicians and the people they serve want to be able to say, "Well, we don't need to uphold the treaties any longer because there aren't any people left on the land who would identify themselves as treaty rights holders."

Despite all those pressures and politics at play in First Nations communities across the country, I've never viewed Serpent River with a jaundiced eye. It's still a place that allows me to feel a type of connection I feel nowhere else. My family is there, and love and happiness are part of the very ground. So, even if I see the scars and damage left by colonialism, my love of the place overrides that view. For me, that unquenchable feeling speaks to the endurance of our people. You put us in a desolate corner of what used to be a grand territory and somehow we'll still make it a place worth loving and returning to, even as you try to grind it down to dust.

CHAPTER 3

My Little Nuisance

The summer after I turned seven I woke up one morning with the worst migraine I'd ever had. Even as a small child I got them. This, though, was something different. The dimmest light turned into piercing blades. Pain shot through my skull in flashes that obliterated thought. Anything but the gentlest movement was nauseating.

I'd had the headache, though not quite as severe, the day before as well. The persistence and worsening of the symptoms were obviously worrying to my parents, and when I told my mom that my neck was stiff, I could feel her concern intensify. She asked me to try to touch my chin to my chest, and I couldn't do it without severe pain. I could barely move my head at all. She and my dad immediately bundled me into the car, and we headed to Sick Kids Hospital in downtown Toronto. I had no idea what the issue was, but from the hurried focus of their movements, I could tell it was urgent.

The drive was quiet, my dad speeding, his attention locked on the road. The only sound was my mother's reassuring voice telling me everything would be all right. Telling me and telling herself.

When we arrived, my dad carried me straight into the emergency room. My parents had called ahead and we were quickly ushered into an examination room, where a friendly doctor entered moments later. He asked me to repeat the chin-to-chest exercise my mom had attempted to run me through earlier, with the same results. He then had me try to turn my head from side to side. That movement was also excruciating. He left the room to speak with my parents as I got changed into a flimsy hospital gown.

When the doctor and my parents returned, three other members of the hospital staff trailed them into the room. They were all big men, and though they looked at me with kind expressions, their mere presence was unsettling. What was wrong with me that required this entire crowd of people to fix it? The doctor told me he needed to perform something called a "spinal tap" so that he could figure out how best to help me. He said it meant I had to get a needle in my back, and I had to keep very still so that the needle would work properly. The orderlies, he told me, were there to help me keep still.

The orderlies took hold of my hands and feet and held tight to me as I lay face down. The doctor didn't give much in the way of a warning before he began, maybe knowing a countdown couldn't help in the slightest. A spinal tap is an invasive procedure in which a massive needle is inserted into your spine to collect a sample of cerebrospinal fluid, the liquid that surrounds and protects your brain. I didn't know that, nor did I see the needle beforehand, but when it entered my back I forgot my headache completely. It was, at that time, the most painful thing I'd ever felt. In fact, the fear and pain burned the experience into my memory so intensely that I seem to have lost many of my memories of the time before that needle was plunged into my seven-year-old back.

Usually the fluid collected in the syringe is sent for laboratory testing before a doctor makes a diagnosis, but my doctor, whose friendliness I was now seriously questioning, took one look at the tinted fluid and ordered the room emptied immediately. When he came back in he was wearing a face mask and completely covered in a long protective gown. The nurse with him was in the same getup, and she put a mask on me.

As I was wheeled to the door, an announcement came over the hospital's P.A. system asking for the hallways to be cleared. I was pushed out of the exam room and then rushed to an elevator, the doctor and nurse on either side yelling for the way to be cleared as people frantically ducked back into their rooms. We rode the elevator up to a floor where the hallways were already pretty clear, and I was wheeled into a private room. My parents then appeared, also dressed in hospital gowns and face masks. I could see in their eyes just how scared for me they were, though they did their best to be strong. My mom told me I had viral meningitis. If I needed any more hints as to how serious my illness was, I needed only to look around the room—everything was wrapped in plastic, including the TV mounted high on the wall. I would spend the next two weeks there.

Although I recovered from the infection in the two weeks I was confined to my hospital room, the meningitis weakened me to the point that it triggered a bout of secondary disaccharidase deficiency, a loss of enzymes crucial for your digestive system to process sugars. I wasn't allowed fruit or most vegetables. A family friend, who suffered from diabetes, managed to locate a sugar-free ginger ale, which became my beverage of choice. This was in 1981, before there was even Diet Coke, so choices were limited. My mother would liven up water with some sort of allowable sweetener, but this was hardly flavour country.

Beyond the physical toll, the illness had a huge mental impact on me. While viral meningitis isn't nearly as dangerous as its bacterial cousin, it's still highly contagious and potentially life altering. In the hospital, the toys I played with were either wrapped in plastic or disposed of after I was done with them. The medical staff I interacted with were similarly shielded, as they would only enter covered head to toe, with surgical masks obscuring their faces. Other than the friendly doctor I'd seen initially, I didn't have much sense of what any of them actually looked like.

My mom and dad were the only visitors allowed into my room. Everyone else had to stand outside and look through a wide window. I could see them, but I couldn't be with them. My parents always put on a brave face for me, but I still picked up on their anxiety, and it amplified my own. I felt like I was trapped in a horrible sci-fi film; I was worried I was going to die. It was terrifying.

To this day I tend to be wary of doctors and hospitals. I spent a fair amount of time in hospitals as a kid, and unlike a young adventurer who lands in the ER with a broken bone, I was never there because of a mishap suffered while doing something fun. Meningitis, disaccharidase deficiency, asthma, a kidney infection—none of this was fun, none of it came from fun, and none of it made me fun. I've been told I can be humourless, and I was described as a serious child. Is there any wonder why? My illnesses were always serious, and they left me both suspicious of life and deeply cautious, as if life itself were a risk. I've never lost the feeling of being trapped behind glass, too sick to even see the outside world, and I have no doubt that my health has and will continue to suffer as a result of my aversion to medical professionals.

Even after I was healthy enough to be taken home from the hospital, I had to spend the summer mostly confined to bed. I couldn't do much of anything but watch our small television, moved into the room I shared with my sister, Maggie. Not, as it turns out, an altogether useless pastime, given that I'd eventually manage to make watching things my career. But I was used to childhood summers where I'd run out the door in the morning, a "Come home when the streetlights turn on" the only stricture put on my day. Being stuck inside drinking sugar-free ginger ales, with only that little TV to keep me company much of the time, made it one of the most miserable summers of my life.

***

When I finally returned to school, I was still weak. I couldn't walk the distance from our house, so I was pushed to class in an old stroller my parents had tucked away in the garage after my sister stopped needing it. Just what every seven-year-old boy wants: showing up for the first day of school in a stroller last used by your kid sister.

Even with that bit of humiliation, though, school was a welcome connection to the outside world, and to normalcy. I couldn't last a full day yet, even if I wasn't exactly exerting myself at recess. One of my parents or my grandmother would arrive with the stroller at lunchtime to pick me up and bring me home. But having come so close to death and having spent so many weeks indoors, it was a relief to see my friends again. And as physically and mentally drained as I was, it was still a pleasure to have something other than daytime television to set my mind to.

As my friend Thomas King has so aptly put it, inconvenience is what turns special needs into a nuisance. My leaving every day at lunch, my turning up in a makeshift wheelchair, my being depleted in a way that occasionally made it hard to engage in class—unbeknownst to me, all these things were grating on my teacher. Maybe she saw my presence as disruptive to the rest of the kids in class; maybe it was my sudden absence every afternoon. Whatever the cause, she started to view the accommodations I needed as an inconvenience. From there, her thinking followed the path Thomas outlined: as the supposed cause of the inconvenience, I was an annoyance, a nuisance.

I know she felt that way because she told me, in front of the entire class.

It was an unremarkable day a couple of months into the school year. I'd been getting gradually stronger, week to week, but that morning I remember feeling that I'd barely be able to manage until my grandmother came to get me. There were still a few minutes left until the lunch bell, but for all intents and purposes the class had finished, so I began packing up my things, getting ready to go home. My teacher asked what I was doing. When I started to explain she shook her head at me, the gesture cutting me off. She waited a moment. Then, in a sickly sweet voice, as though it were a term of endearment, she said, "You're my little nuisance. You know that?"

One of the most harrowing times of my life had made me a problem in the eyes of an adult who should've had my best interests at heart. It wasn't the first way the public school system had failed me, but, for my mother, it was the final straw.

Residential schools like the one my *nookomis* was forced to attend came with graveyards instead of libraries. Their mandate was to erase Indigeneity through coercion while preparing students for a life of servitude and, at best, second-class citizenry. The larger system that supported these schools ripped children from their families and communities; physically, sexually, and emotionally abused them; murdered them; left them shattered and robbed of the most fundamental aspects of their cultural identities.

Mainstream Canada frames the violence of the residential school system as a thing of the past, an unfortunate mistake captured in grainy black-and-white photographs and handwritten letters. We are to believe that this elaborate and intentional program of eradication was the product of a different, unenlightened society. We are to believe that this country has learned empathy, remorse, and humanity. We are to believe that its crimes are distant memories. The fact that residential schools were still in existence in 1996 is a fact glossed over. But even today, as outlined in Tanya Talaga's essential book *Seven Fallen Feathers*, Indigenous children are often removed from their families in order to attend school. Is the uprooting of First Nations, Métis, and Inuit kids today as nefarious as it was when it was done by institutions like St. Joseph's School for Girls? No, most certainly not. But all too often, the results are distressingly similar.

While many school boards have taken to heart the recommendations of the Truth and Reconciliation Commission, and many individual teachers have worked hard to find ways to bring those recommendations into the classroom in meaningful ways, there has still been little done to shift the nature of education to better reflect First Nations, Métis, and Inuit values. Outcomes for Indigenous children within the colonial educational system remain far below those of their white peers. In a report released in 2015, Andrew Parkin, an education researcher, found that the gap between white and Indigenous students in educational achievement—measured by the highest level of education reached—had actually widened since the mid-1990s. In 1996, the gap between the percentage of Indigenous people with university degrees and non-Indigenous people with the same level of education was twelve points; by 2011, it was up to seventeen, even though both groups graduated more total students.

A primary reason for the gap in educational outcomes is the disparity in many other areas of life. Indigenous kids are far more likely to live in poverty than their white peers, far more likely to lack access to clean drinking water, and far more likely to have families scarred by their experiences with the educational system in previous generations. Is it really any wonder that the children and grandchildren of people who were tortured in school grow up with a distrust of and aversion to those same institutions?

The fundamental betrayal of education that residential schools represent is further compounded by what many First Nations, Métis, and Inuit parents believed when they sent their kids to places like St. Joseph's voluntarily. My great-grandparents thought they were providing their children with an avenue to success and acceptance within the broader Canadian culture and society. They believed the attractive lie residential schools were selling: that attendance offered a chance to learn and integrate. When they made those decisions, my great-grandparents had already seen much of their way of life destroyed. Alex had trapped furs for the Hudson's Bay Company, but that means of supporting himself and his family was disappearing, along with most of the other avenues available to Indigenous people. What better way to set up their children for success in this new nation than to teach them its ways?

That broken trust still resonates. And how could it not? There has never been any meaningful effort to restore it. The system still fails us and, intentional or not, the effects are the same.

Solutions exist, many of them outlined in easily accessible public documents like the TRC's Final Report, the Final Report of the National Inquiry into Missing and Murdered Indigenous Women and Girls, and the Report of the Royal Commission on Aboriginal Peoples. But few of these have been truly put into practice, and most are, at best, mid-term fixes. The failure of the educational system is multigenerational, and this poses a barrier to its own evolution that is rarely addressed. While it's true that the education my children receive around the history of Canada and its relationship with Indigenous people is more complete than the one I was provided, the curriculum is still largely being taught by people who learned as I did. And indeed, we can see how that failure of education plays out in our civic life: the media fails to even grasp Indigenous issues, let alone fully reflect them, and those who govern us continue to drag their feet in implementing change.

Murray Sinclair, now-retired senator and commissioner of the TRC, has rightly declared that "education got us into this mess and education will get us out of it," but the pace of that change means many more will be harmed while we wait. What is needed, of course, is a vast investment of resources, but any significant increase in funding is complicated by Canada's own governance and how it manages the relationship between First Nations, Métis, and Inuit and the state. Education isn't the only system administered this way, but it's a prime example of how an invented bureaucracy serves to further harm Indigenous children. Whereas schooling for non-Indigenous children is a provincial or territorial responsibility, schooling for First Nations, Métis, and Inuit kids is a federal service. This reflects the fact that the treaty relationship is almost always established between nations and the federal state or the monarchy itself. And since we're the only population that the federal government serves in this way, its infrastructure to administer education nationally isn't nearly as neat as that of the provinces. This can—and often does—leave an Indigenous kid without the same resources or level of services as a white kid one town over.

Like so many issues that exist between First Nations, Métis, and Inuit and the Canadian state, the most crucial step toward resolution lies in sovereignty. Education, as Indigenous communities understood it, was always meant to be an exchange between cultures—we learn your ways, you learn some of ours. It was never meant to encourage dominion of one over the other, and yet colonial governments deployed it as one of their many methods to disenfranchise, oppress, and dominate. And as Sinclair has pointed out, since education was used to attack Indigenous sovereignty, it should also be used to reinforce it. Key to that would be allowing communities to build and operate their own schools with their own curricula, resourced at a level consistent with that of the best-funded public schools in the country.

Some examples of this approach, such as in Manitoba's Norway House Cree Nation, have produced encouraging results—graduating more students while also infusing the existing curriculum with teachings from the Indigenous community. Allowing the community to decide how best to educate its young people in this way is essential to easing and eventually undoing the harm the Canadian education system has inflicted on Indigenous people.

Yet despite the inspiring successes of these hybrid models, we must also acknowledge that the Canadian style of education may not offer a true solution. University, a deeply colonial idea and institution, is simply not the ideal path for many Indigenous people. My family saw it as perhaps the pinnacle of academic achievement, since so few of our Anishinaabe relatives ever pursued it. But university is simply one path among many for life- and career-building. What we encourage children to pursue should be what's best for them as individual people, not what simply seems to have worked for everyone else.

The nuns at St. Joseph's saw my grandmother's ultimate potential as little more than a servant or secretary. How many white people would support an institution that put such limits on their child? So it should come as no surprise that Indigenous people still struggle within an educational system largely designed to strip them of their identity and culture. Yes, the shameful underfunding of the rural schools that serve our communities is part of the problem here, but even when Indigenous children attend better resourced and maintained schools in the city, they still tend to perform at a lower level than their non-Indigenous classmates. The system fails them wherever they engage with it, from coast to coast to coast.

When it was time to send my own children to school, there were few attractive options. My wife and I didn't want to send them to private school, which was mostly a moot point since we couldn't afford the tuition anyway. Our son and daughter both have exceptionalities that require additional supports. So we started out hoping to build a relationship with a local school centred on Indigenous children, putting both of them into a pre-kindergarten program meant to help kids prepare for school while offering Indigenous-led childcare. They would be surrounded by other First Nations kids, within an environment designed to cater to them. We thought it ideal.

Shortly after they joined pre-kindergarten, though, the program director told my wife that she thought our four-year-old son would never lead an independent life. She'd known him for only a couple of weeks, but she apparently felt comfortable making such a final assessment. We were devastated. Not because we believed her or agreed with her, but because it felt as though that judgment would influence how he was treated. And it did. We were called several times to come get him before the day was over. There seemed little patience for him and for the problem-solving that might have made the program more welcoming.

Instead, the solution always seemed to be to just have him removed.

It was then that we realized how much we'd have to advocate for our children, even within an educational setting meant to serve First Nations children. Over the years we've sought out experts to work with our kids, and to assess them so that we'd have the necessary diagnoses and documentation to get them the supports they need in school. This often meant paying for assessments out of pocket instead of waiting on a list to receive them, and then pushing the school board and principals to make the accommodations necessary for our children to feel comfortable at school. It also meant us moving. We realized early on that, as much as we loved our small home in the city's east end, the schools in our neighbourhood simply weren't going to work for our kids. My parents happen to live in one of the best public school districts in Toronto, and since our kids arrived my mother had driven across town nearly every day to help us—an hour each way, through heavy traffic. Ultimately, then, we decided to move about a fifteen-minute walk from my parents' in the west end. It shouldn't be surprising when I tell you that our new neighbourhood is home to both more wealth and more white people than where we moved from. Where affluence and whiteness congregate, systems meant to support everyone suddenly do a better job of it.

Now, as my daughter enters high school, albeit with her first year disrupted by the pandemic, she's exactly where she dreamed: at a big high school in a specialized arts program, and with enough supports that we feel confident she can excel. Our son is now in grade eight in the gifted program. They still have their exceptionalities, and they still require accommodations, but we advocate for them constantly and, so far, we think we've managed to help them succeed where others thought they would fail. But it's not lost on me that this sort of advocacy is a privilege that requires enormous energy and time—and occasionally expense. My wife is a lawyer and I'm a professional communicator. What about the parents who can't advocate in this way, or this effectively? What about the parents who can't use their economic privilege to pay for supports their children might not otherwise receive? What about families that can't move to other neighbourhoods in order to access better schooling? I worry that these parents and their children are harmed needlessly and may never find the supports they need.

There are efforts now to introduce Indigenous ways of knowing and a more accurate history of this country into curricula across Canada. The Truth and Reconciliation Commission's focus on education has been effective in mobilizing school boards and teachers—many of whom, to their credit, have long been eager to implement this material in their classrooms—even if that movement has clashed with the policies set forth by provincial governments. This is important work, but it's largely meant to serve a non-Indigenous population. And while it's crucial to the advancement of Indigenous peoples that non-Indigenous Canadians gain a better understanding of our joint history and issues, it's even more important that the method of educating Indigenous peoples changes.

Indigenous kids shouldn't have to conform, to sacrifice who they are, to get an education. Period. They shouldn't have to move away from their families, either. Indigenous communities should have schools nearby, and those communities should be given the support and autonomy to determine how to educate their children in a way that best serves those kids and their communities. First Nations schools should be shining examples of the absolute best our public education system can provide, with rested and thoughtful teachers, resources to accommodate any special need, and all the latest technology. This would acknowledge and address, in some part, both the history of education's weaponization against Indigenous peoples and the share of Canadian wealth that should be apparent in First Nations, Métis, and Inuit communities. For the entirety of its existence, the education system in Canada has failed FNMI kids and their parents, or worse. We must cut a different path.

***

When my mom got home from work that night, she noticed that I seemed upset and asked what was wrong. I told her what the teacher had called me. Boy, was she pissed.

Looking back, especially with the added perspective of having kids of my own, I know that her anger had been building for a long time. My mom had herself been a teacher, and she'd long known that I needed special attention I wasn't getting in class. On my first-term report card that year, which arrived shortly before the nuisance comment, I'd received straight A's, but I still couldn't read. How could I be a top student when I was falling behind my classmates in such a fundamental area?

I can't know that my Indigeneity had anything to do with the way my teacher treated me, only that being an Indigenous kid in a Canadian school opens you up to all manner of mistreatment and inattention. The education system in this country has yet to run out of ways to fail and harm Indigenous kids, just as the colonial structures that underlie it have yet to run out of ways to damage and dispossess our communities. The way I was failed was just one drop in that big, ugly bucket.

My mom had been on the parent-teacher council the whole time my sister and I were in school, and she was its president that year. She was engaged and well-positioned to make herself heard to teachers and school administrators. But, as so many parents of marginalized children and children with any kind of special needs will know firsthand, being an informed and dedicated advocate doesn't guarantee that you'll be able to effect the change your kid needs. So many parents talk themselves hoarse and run themselves ragged fighting with our public education system. Our challenges and the lengths my parents went to, then, were sadly common things, as was my mom's desire to find something better for us. But unlike many others in that situation, we had other options. We weren't trapped. And after I came home that day and told her about the blatant way my teacher had made her feelings for me known, my mom made up her mind to make that turn.

CHAPTER 4

The Other Half

The year after my brush with death, when I'd almost fully recovered from meningitis and disaccharidase deficiency, my mother pulled my sister and me out of the public system and put us in private school. She chose Montcrest School, which was housed in an old mansion on the east side of Toronto, down a small dead-end street off Broadview Avenue with a terrific view of the Don Valley. It was a different world, with classes held in what were once bedrooms and studies, and usually with fewer than twenty students per class.

My sister and I started at the same time, Maggie in grade two and me in grade three. The smaller class sizes meant teachers were much more attentive and involved with each student—surprise, surprise—and in addition to the regular schoolwork I was plunged into intensive phonics courses in order to get me reading. That occurred in record time, confirming to my parents that public school had utterly failed us and that they'd made the right decision in opting for the private stream, even if it was very expensive.

Tuition at Montcrest was tens of thousands of dollars a year, an insurmountable barrier for most families. And back in the mid-eighties, my parents didn't have that kind of money either. Like the down payment for our house in East York, my school fees were paid for by my paternal grandparents.

My dad was born and spent the earliest years of his life in Evanston, Illinois, a wealthy suburb on the north side of Chicago. His father, Bill, was a navy veteran who'd served in the South Pacific during the Second World War, which helps explain how he later became a harbour master. His mother, Barbara, was a pharmaceutical executive. In 1964 or '65, when my dad was about twelve, my grandparents' marriage fell apart. My grandmother moved to Toronto to live with another man, taking my dad and his sisters, Margaret and Sally, along with her. Barbara was successful in her own right, and her second husband, Tom, was an engineer with an expanding practice. So while my mom's mother worked at the Albany Club, my dad's parents were members of the Royal Canadian Yacht Club. They're the source of much of the privilege I've accessed in my life.

Because of the distance, Maggie and I had to take the subway to Montcrest, which gave me my first real taste of independence. After school we'd go to my maternal grandparents' place until my mom or dad could pick us up. There, my grandfather Jack, a large man with a shock of white hair and a big round belly, would dote on us, excitedly hurrying us into the house for Cheezies or pancakes.

At school, as the increased attention worked its magic and I improved academically, I also began to discover new passions. The drama teacher— a kind, wonderfully supportive man named Seamus Caulfield, who doubled as the shop instructor—was the first adult to encourage my artistic self, and in his drama class I became obsessed with acting. The school plays he directed were staged in a large conjoined room on the mansion's first floor, what had once been the living room and dining room. Seamus cast me in central roles in two productions, and made a point of impressing on me that he believed I possessed real talent. He even went so far as to refer me to an agent he knew.

I was eleven when my mother brought me to the introductory meeting. Before that she'd found a photographer to take my headshot, and in that headshot my hair was regulation short and neat. At Montcrest—and later Crescent, where I'd go to high school—the boys' dress code included strict guidelines about hair, a faint echo of the forced haircuts my grandmother had endured at St. Joseph's and intended to achieve the same goal: conformity. But at the agent's, that haircut quickly became a sticking point. After my mother and I sat down, the agent laid out the hard truth in a "Let me level with you" tone of voice.

"Well, if you really want to work steadily," she said, "you're going to have to grow your hair and go out for Native roles."

I had no idea what that meant. Aside from *The Beachcombers* and the old westerns I occasionally watched on TV, I'd never seen an Indigenous person in a dramatic role on screen, and neither of those options seemed like a steady source of work for an eleven-year-old. I looked to my mom for clarification, but I could tell from her expression that she wasn't willing to engage with the idea. I was just about to resign myself to a life of obscurity when the agent, flipping through a stack of scripts and casting call notices, told us that she might actually have something for me. A TV show was looking for a large group of kids to appear in a single episode, so she arranged to send me on the audition.

The program was *The Ray Bradbury Theater*, an American production that initially aired on HBO and featured the famous author of *Fahrenheit 451* himself introducing dramatizations of his short stories à la *Alfred Hitchcock Presents*. When my mom and I arrived at the designated time, the place was swarming with kids, many of them veterans of the audition process. Seeing their professionalism—or what I took to be professionalism at the time—I assumed I probably wouldn't get a part. I didn't know what I was doing; I just enjoyed performing. I decided to just give it a shot anyway and try to learn anything I could.

When a woman with a clipboard called out my name I was led into a long, narrow room with a conference table running down its middle. A handful of adults were seated around the table. One of them announced that the star of the episode was going to be William Shatner.

I may have had only a vague understanding of who Ray Bradbury was, but William Shatner? Now there was a name I knew. Shatner played Captain Kirk, and I'd seen every episode of *Star Trek* by then, plus the original film in theatres. He was also T.J. Hooker, the TV cop. In the span of a few seconds I went from thinking of the audition as over before it began to really, really wanting a part.

They gave me a single line to deliver, and I can remember it to this day (impressed?): "Welcome back to the playground, Charlie." I repeated it for the casting people several times. The role was a villainous bully, so I did my best to sound menacing and a bit unhinged. Then they asked me to act as though I were transforming into an animal. Yes, I growled. Hey, a chance to meet William Shatner was on the line. I was committed.

I left the room not knowing whether I'd had a good audition or a terrible one, still not sure of what constituted a good audition. My effort, it turned out, had been at least of fair quality: I got a part.

It wasn't the main part I'd read for—I wouldn't have any lines—but I was more than an extra. My character even had a name, Bully #3. Okay, that's more of a designation than a name, but at least I was credited; I wasn't just a random kid on the playground. That was the name of the episode, "The Playground." Shatner starred as a man who was bullied as a kid and so is plagued by anxiety when he sends his own son to the same playground where he'd been tormented. His younger self was played by an established child actor, who the other kids told me had starred as Mikey in the "Mikey likes it!" Life cereal ads. I was in heady company.

My mom took a week off work so she could drive me to the set every day and remain there as my guardian, as each kid had to be accompanied by an adult. We had to bring our own wardrobe, which was supposed to look timeless, allowing us to be both kids of the present and kids of the past. The playground set, with its background of building facades, was inside a sound stage. We would shoot for a couple hours at a time and then take a break.

In my big scene, I stood in a row with Bully #1 and Bully #2 as we threatened the adult Shatner, who'd been transferred to his son's body—as happens from time to time. We bullies had to look intimidating while balling our hands into menacing fists. Then we swarmed the monkey bars and beat up our victim. I can't say my performance was award-worthy, but the whole experience was thrilling. I even made some on-set friends, including a couple of the actors who'd go on to star in *Degrassi Junior High*. On the last day of shooting, Shatner generously posed for a picture with each of us. In mine, he wrapped an arm around my neck as if I were in a patented T.J. Hooker chokehold.

As much as I loved it, my first professional acting role was also my last. When the *Degrassi* auditions came up a short while later, I was disappointed that I didn't get sent. Imagine how different my life would have been if I'd landed a part on that show. I could have been the Indigenous kid who has all sorts of issues! Just think of the potential story arcs.

My agent never sent me to another audition. I didn't follow her advice and grow my hair out. Maybe that alone made me uncastable: too Indigenous to play a "normal" kid, not Indigenous enough for the "Native" roles. It was an uncomfortable middle ground, one I'd become more familiar with as I got older.

It should boggle the mind that being judged fit to appear on screen depended on the length of my hair, but it's not even particularly surprising. If an Indian turns up in a TV show or movie—it doesn't matter when or where it's set, it doesn't matter when or where it was made—that Indian has long hair. It's a trope so established that, in Hollywood, when a casting agent can't find any Indigenous people with long hair, it's up to the wardrobe department to manufacture some. In many 1950s westerns, the Indians wore headbands, not because it was culturally accurate (it almost never was), but rather to keep the wigs from falling off their heads—a particular challenge given that so much of the action took place on horseback.

This can seem funny at first blush, but it's actually tragic. Tragic because to the industry that shapes so much of the way we view the world, the only Indian worth portraying is the one with long hair who dies, either nobly (read: aiding a white protagonist) or in villainy (read: resisting a white protagonist). It doesn't matter which, so long as they die.

I've met people whose view of the world was so shaped by this misinformation that they believed all Indians were dead, that we'd gone extinct. I've met others who refused to believe I was Indigenous because I didn't have long hair. The enduring stereotype that ended my fledgling acting career, along with the lack of any other Indigenous representation, has narrowed people's understanding of Indigenous life and of what an Indigenous person looks like down to this one image, as thin as a culturally inaccurate headband.

The headbands were also tragic because one of the reasons so many Indigenous actors wore their hair short was that it coincided with the peak of assimilationist policies in both Canada and the United States. Sometimes our hair was cut forcibly, as my grandmother's was; other times we cut our hair as a way to fit in, to assert and embrace modernity. Cutting our hair has always been a method of control and erasure, and the depiction of Indigenous people only with long hair is part of the framework that makes that control and erasure possible.

I've appeared on screen plenty of times since my week with William Shatner, but I never acted again. I did, though, go to meet one other agent. By then I was in university and needed work. I remembered how much fun I'd had acting and thought it might be worth a second attempt. So I got another headshot taken—one my wife, Julie, teasingly refers to as my "bedroom eyes" photo—and took it with me to my meeting.

When I arrived, I handed over the headshot. The agent looked at it, looked up at me, and looked back at the headshot.

"If you really want to work," he said, "you'll have to grow your hair."

CHAPTER 5

Empire Strikes Pretty Much Continuously

My love of acting led me to school productions and one thrilling week of work with William Shatner; my love of movies would give me the driving passion of my professional life.

I was three when my parents took me to the University Theatre on Bloor Street to see *Star Wars*, the movie everyone was talking about. My mom had already bought me a vinyl record with portions of its audio and I'd listened to it endlessly, memorizing long stretches of dialogue and even the accompanying sound effects. *Maybe*, my mom eventually thought, *he'd like to see the whole thing*.

It was the first movie I'd seen in a theatre and I was mesmerized, right from the opening moments (that massive spaceship flying overhead and into the frame) to the final scene (the celebratory award ceremony on Yavin 4). *Star Wars* was revolutionary. There had never been anything like it. If it doesn't inspire the same awe today, that's in large part because its visual language and soundscapes have found their echo in most of the movies made in modern Hollywood. Of course, three-year-old me had no idea of the movie's place in cinematic history. I just loved everything about it. I wanted the lunchboxes, the bedsheets, the comic books, the pyjamas, the posters, the Obi-Wan Kenobi with Double-Telescoping Lightsaber—everything I could get my hands on. I have now seen the original more than 280 times. I still love it, and the passion it inspired in me went beyond that one franchise.

From the moment that iconic opening crawl began—my mom leaning close to my ear in the theatre to read it to me, "It is a period of civil war . . ."—movies were what excited me most. Fortunately, my mom also loved them, and she was happy to indulge me. Every week-end we'd watch *Saturday Night at the Movies* hosted by Elwy Yost, a weekly presentation of classic films with accompanying interviews and essay segments. Curled up together on the couch, my mom and I would watch whatever came on, from gritty noir to Fred Astaire danc-ing across the ceiling.

My parents were extremely permissive in what they let me watch. The only two things they didn't want me to see were the TV show *Three's Company* (I remain grateful for that) and the Canadian-made sex comedy *Porky's*. Of course, the fact that they were forbidden imme-diately made them the most important items on my to-do list. I watched *Porky's* at a friend's house shortly after my parents had banned it. I was about nine and really didn't get what the big deal was; nudity wasn't much of a priority for me. Girls didn't attract my attention the way movies did until I was well into my teenage years, and even then, they only really got equal billing if a date involved a night out at the theatre.

As relaxed as my parents were in what they let me watch, my mom was an early believer in the importance of media literacy for kids. She made sure I knew that what was on screen was fake, and would ask me questions about anything we watched together, gauging my under-standing and sounding out my opinions. She didn't pressure or quiz me; she just showed real interest in the films and what I thought about them.

I often felt we were discovering and exploring deeper layers of meaning together. In that way, my education in movies started in my house, watching them on TV, with my mom as my teacher.

My obsession was so all-encompassing that most of my playtime was movie-focused, or at least movie-themed. My cousin Sean was also a movie geek, so when we played in the yard it wasn't Cops and Robbers or Cowboys and Indians, it was Logan's Run or, of course, Star Wars. My G.I. Joes were forever recast as rebel fighters and soldiers of the empire, or post-apocalyptic survivors from the world of *Mad Max*, or replicants from *Blade Runner*, or soon-to-be-snacks for *Alien*'s xenomorph. Even my favourite stuffed animal, a penguin I got for Christmas in 1978, couldn't escape the lure of life on set. Danger Eagle, as he came to be known, was defined by his willingness to engage in death-defying behaviour other stuffies shied away from. Whether it was a tumble down the basement stairs or a risky leap off my bed, he was up for anything.

Danger Eagle was my way of participating in a world like the one I'd seen in *The Muppet Movie*, the only other film with a place in my heart to rival the one occupied by *Star Wars*. I had no idea how to make puppets like the ones that sprang from Jim Henson's amazing imagination (and equally amazing workshop), but a penguin stunt bird was, for me, a character that could have plausibly appeared alongside the Muppets.

These adventures also led me to try to figure out what it took to make a movie. Spurred on by my mom's curiosity, I'd always been willing to investigate why I liked a movie or a particular character and what I found boring or compelling in a film's plot and presentation. By age ten or eleven, though, a new question started to occupy more of my thoughts: *How? How do they do that? How was that made?* I wanted to understand the process of filmmaking.

My education was a haphazard one. Even as I got older and my inquiries, interest, and efforts became more sophisticated, I could never see a clear path to a career in the film industry. Certainly the scarcity of Indigenous filmmakers to model myself after played into that, a lack compounded by the fact that the Canadian industry was still in its infancy and there weren't many homegrown success stories to be inspired by.

As teenagers, my friends and I attempted to learn by doing, shooting original short films with whatever technology was available. The most memorable of these was a zombie movie my friend Tal Zimerman and I planned to shoot over the course of a weekend with the help of our classmates Steve Munro and David Scott.

Tal and I shared a love of horror movies and the gruesome makeup effects that lived within them, created by geniuses like Tom Savini, Rick Baker, and Stan Winston. For our blockbuster—really just a single epic scene in which a zombie would break in through a window to feast on an unsuspecting victim lying in bed—we planned to use a trick we'd picked up after watching a documentary on Savini, the renowned special effects artist best known for his work on several of George A. Romero's horror classics. For Romero's *Dawn of the Dead*, the documentary explained, Savini had used real animal entrails for many of the most visceral scenes. Tal and I decided that following the same course would take our movie to a whole new level.

We were shooting at Tal's house, our supply of entrails sourced from a local butcher and wrapped in brown paper packages in his family's fridge. Just before filming, we pulled the packages out along with the other ingredients for our intestinal stew and began assembling it all on the kitchen counter. It was at that point that Tal's grandfather walked in.

Unbeknownst to me, Tal's family kept a kosher kitchen, meaning our display represented a gross violation of their religious beliefs. When Tal's grandfather, dressed in a black suit with his grey hair falling in perfect curls down each side of his face, saw what we were up to, his face turned ashen. He then exploded, yelling in what I would later figure out was Yiddish.

Tal's response was frantic and also in Yiddish, but it was crystal clear that our shoot was in deep jeopardy. Amazingly, though, whatever Tal said, it worked—at least to the extent that his grandfather turned and stormed out of the room. We cleaned the kitchen, gathered up the entrails, and made our way out back to film the grisly scene.

Tragically, the result has not survived. Tal did, however, go on to become a filmmaker. His documentary, *Why Horror?*—in which I make an appearance to discuss our mutual love of scary movies—came out in 2014.

When I got older, my movie-watching would more frequently take me out of the house. I'd venture up the hill to the Golden Mile Theatre to catch classics like *Gymkata*, a martial arts-meets-gymnastics action flick that lasted all of one day in cinemas. I'd head downtown to the newly opened multiplex in the Eaton Centre to see the top blockbusters as well as the occasional piece of 3-D silliness like *Metalstorm: The Destruction of Jared-Syn*, a cheap Mad Max knockoff that I nonetheless watched several times in one of the multiplex's small, smelly theatres. At the Warden Woods Mall I'd see many of the movies that impacted me most, from *Die Hard* to a double billing of *Star Wars* and *The Empire Strikes Back* when the sequel was released in 1980. Later, when I could drive and borrow my mom's Honda Civic, I'd become a regular at the Fox Theatre on Queen Street East.

Every time I went out to the movies or hit the VCR's play button I was, on some level, chasing the exhilaration I felt when I first saw *Star Wars* back in 1977. That pursuit still drives me—but there's a second feeling I find myself trying to return to as well. Curled up on the couch with my mom, marvelling at Myrna Loy and William Powell's razor-sharp, booze-soaked banter in the *Thin Man* movies or Gene Kelly's umbrella-twirling dance number in *Singin' in the Rain* or Bette Davis's spinster-to-knockout metamorphosis in *Now, Voyager*, I felt a perfect childhood mix of warmth, comfort, security, and love. That earliest film school wasn't only engaging and interesting; it was also the first place I learned that I could hold someone's attention with the things I thought and felt about movies.

My deep love of movies truly needed those emotional touchstones, because the films themselves didn't always have much to offer an Indigenous person. As my brief acting career had highlighted, representation of First Nations, Métis, and Inuit people on screen was almost nonexistent. Hollywood wasn't built as an educational project; it's a dream factory, and in particular an American Dream factory, churning out the myths that underpin the white picket fence, the two and a half kids, the new car in the garage. There wasn't much place in that dream for us, apparently.

Outside the reductive and destructive confines of a western, the sight of an Indigenous person on TV or in a movie was such a rare occurrence when I was a kid that I can remember each one individually. There was Jesse Jim, played by Pat John, on *The Beachcombers*, and there was Buffy Sainte-Marie's appearance on *Sesame Street*. That's about it.

That scarcity is part of the reason Alanis Obomsawin's film *Incident at Restigouche* made such a huge impression on me when I first saw it on the CBC in the mid-eighties. The other part is its raw and revolutionary power. *Incident at Restigouche* is a forty-minute documentary chronicling a clash over fishing rights between the Mi'kmaq in Restigouche—what's now called Listuguj First Nation in eastern Quebec, just north of the New Brunswick border—and local white fishermen. The Mi'kmaq community had set up a peaceful blockade and, in return, had seen some of their boats burned and a government response that involved raids by armed provincial police officers.

I was ten or so when I saw it, and beyond there being a clear division between the government and First Nations, I'm not sure I understood what the central conflict was about. What really struck me about the movie was Obomsawin herself. *Incident at Restigouche* was the first of her films in which she appeared. There's a famous scene in which she interviews Lucien Lessard, the Quebec minister of fisheries who'd ordered the raids on Listuguj. In their exchange, Obomsawin is self-possessed, sure of her knowledge and the righteousness of her convictions, and so passionate that she's even aggressive at times.

It was significant enough to see an Indigenous person who wasn't covered in war paint and riding a horse. But here was a woman who looked like my mom, like my grandmother—who looked like family—confronting a powerful agent of colonialism and winning, armed with nothing more than her words and her camera to expose the truth of the situation. As someone who's studied the history of cinema, and of Indigenous cinema in particular, I can say with certainty that it was a groundbreaking event for an Indigenous woman to speak to a government minister like that on camera. You just didn't see it. But because of Alanis Obomsawin, I did.

I remember being even more struck by the realization that the movie was hers, that she had created it, and that it was unlike any other movie I'd known. Indigenous cinema barely existed in Canada in the early 1980s; what little was made was mostly made by Obomsawin. To make a film like *Incident at Restigouche* took superhuman determination. It was, in some ways, a miracle that it existed at all. Yet it didn't make me think of the long odds, of the unlikelihood of ever replicating what Obomsawin had accomplished; instead, it made me hopeful. Here was proof that we could make movies, that it wasn't impossible. Here was proof that a movie could say something other than what they always seemed to say—particularly about Indigenous life. Here was proof that you could use film to tell a story I hadn't been aware of and that, without Obomsawin, I might have believed no one wanted to hear.

Movies didn't have to be pure entertainment. They could have loftier goals. Indigenous people didn't have to be the savages, the villains, the losers. We could instead be the voices of reason, the heroes, the winners. Alanis Obomsawin taught me those things. They have long sustained me and informed much of what I do.

CHAPTER 6

"Go Back to Oka"

Walking through the doors of Crescent School on my first day of grade seven, I made history before I even found my homeroom class: I was the first Indigenous student ever to attend the school, which had been founded in 1913. It was 1986 and Crescent was then what it is now, a boys' private school situated on a thirty-acre estate in one of the most expensive neighbourhoods in Toronto.

In addition to the vast sums of money my grandparents had agreed to pay in tuition, that groundbreaking walk to my first class came only after a rigorous admissions process, a combination job interview and sales pitch. The pitch from the school to my parents, which centred on the fact that Crescent sent 99 percent of its graduates on to university, had been effective. I wasn't the academic sure thing my sister Maggie was, and they probably thought I needed all the help I could get. The interview, presumably meant to determine whether I was worthy of donning the uniform, had gone well enough to establish that I'd fit in—even despite the, you know, seventy-five years of Indigenous exclusion.

In many ways, I did fit in at Crescent. It was a great school, with wonderful facilities and teachers who were, for the most part, engaged and caring educators. School is an uncomfortable place for many Indigenous youth in Canada, even an unbearable one. I was tremendously lucky to go somewhere that gave me the support and encouragement to succeed academically, especially considering my early struggles in the public system.

In other ways, though, I couldn't have felt more out of place. My classmates at Montcrest were privileged kids, but I'd never been conscious of being surrounded by wealth in the way I was at Crescent. Maybe it was a high schooler's increased awareness of such things, but the signifiers of class—and the feeling of being assessed on their basis—hit you before you even entered the school itself. Crescent's main building was, like Montcrest, an old converted mansion. In the front was a large circular driveway where parents and parents' drivers dropped off and picked up their charges. A typical morning involved a parade of luxury cars unloading students. When I first started at Crescent my dad would drop me off in his '85 Chevette. That was never a proud moment, and was something commented on by my wealthier classmates. I was beyond relieved when he eventually bought a new Mazda 626, the family car one less thing about me that might be noticed and ridiculed.

Of course, there were things setting me apart that weren't as fleeting or mutable as an automobile, things I was proud of and didn't want to change. Although Crescent attracted students from all over the world— its distinctly British colonial presentation perhaps appealing as a faster route to assimilation—the student population was overwhelmingly white. Every year maybe ten or twelve people of colour would be divided among the school's internal houses, all named for colonial "heroes" like William Lyon Mackenzie, the explorer Henry Hudson, and British general James Wolfe, as though the sorting hat from *Harry Potter* had been replaced with a pith helmet. I'd always been the only

Indigenous kid in class or on the team, and was occasionally singled out for it, just as I'd been on the Topham Park ball diamond. But in high school, for the first time in a real and lasting way, I started to feel that difference intensely. Sometimes it made me feel excluded or attacked or othered, but slowly it also made me want to better understand my Indigenous identity. I wouldn't have used those words or even thought of it that way at the time, and yet during those years I'd gradually come to recognize that non-Indigenous people would always try to define me from the outside and reduce me to a stereotype. I had access to my fair share of privilege, but I didn't have the white person's luxury of being allowed to simply exist as myself; I'd always be seen through the lens of my Indigeneity. I could let others decide what that meant, or I could discover the answer on my own. I resolved to define myself.

I don't mean that I sat down at my desk one day and wrote "Figure out what it means to you to be an Indigenous person" on a piece of paper. The process of discovery was intentional, but it wasn't always fully conscious, and it was gradual. I'd stumble across an idea, a moment, in music or film or a book that spoke to me, that shone a light on something about myself I'd known but hadn't been able to put a name to, and I clung to those things. I was desperate to feel a connection to someone, or a group of someones, who understood what it was to be othered and who could explain what resistance to that might look and feel like. Later in life I would feel the strongest connections to Indigenous art and thought, but in high school it was hip-hop culture, rap music, and a Black barbershop that first made me feel truly seen.

Although I had white friends at Crescent, I always felt closer to my Black classmates, friends who were themselves greatly outnumbered and marked by difference. We'd swap albums and go to concerts together, and after we became really tight they took me downtown to get my hair cut at the barbershop they all frequented at Dupont and Bathurst streets.

At first I went because I was looking for a way to rebel and, being a teenager, a new hairstyle seemed like one of my better options. The most obvious choice would have been to grow it long, as is the tradition for men in many First Nations. But Crescent's uniform guidelines ruled that out. So instead I got my hair buzzed short, with a design cut into the back.

I loved the barbershop. It felt like a community to me, tight-knit but welcoming in a way that larger society never was. There was always music playing—good music—and the conversation crackled with fun and energy, pulling in or playfully pushing away every person in the room. And there was an acceptance for a Native kid, a feeling that they didn't care I was an Indian but that they deeply cared at the same time.

In that chair, under the apron with the sound of clippers buzzing around me, I could talk sports or movies and laugh my ass off, or I could discuss what it felt like to be treated differently because of my race and know that even the subtlest example would be understood. I felt natural there, comfortable in a way I'd only ever felt in Serpent River. At that time in my life it was a rare and powerful thing to feel seen and supported, and it helped me get through some of the uglier moments at Crescent. To this day, I remain thankful for the kindness I was shown in that shop.

In September 1990, as I returned to Crescent for grade eleven, the Oka Crisis in southwest Quebec was entering its eighth week. That summer the Kanien'kehá:ka from Kahnesatake had erected barricades among the pines of their traditional territory to halt a golf course expansion that would destroy the forest—the latest violation by colonial powers in a land dispute that had been ongoing for decades. On July 11, Quebec's provincial police force had sent in a tactical unit to raid the blockade, firing tear gas and concussion grenades at those gathered in peaceful protest. The situation escalated into a full-fledged gun battle, during which an officer was hit by a bullet and killed. A little more than a month later, after First Nations people across the country had staged actions in support of the Kanien'kehá:ka, the army was brought in.

The Oka Crisis galvanized me. I was sixteen and very conscious of the fact that my family and my community were on "the other side," facing off against the government and seen by the vast majority of Canadians as, if not the enemy, then at least an unsympathetic inconvenience. Meanwhile, suburban Montrealers burned Mohawks in effigy. Neither the violence nor the animosity in that standoff was new—both are older than Canada—but I was shocked and shaken. It was one thing to see us framed as criminal savages in black-and-white westerns, but here it was on the national news.

And then it was in my classroom. The teacher was calling out names for attendance, and when my name came up the kid behind me said, "Go back to Oka."

The boy who told me to go back to a community to which I didn't belong and where I'd never been was South Asian. Born into wealth, limited in both athleticism and humour, he was a scholastic achiever but a bit of a social outsider. He wasn't the least popular kid in school, but he had undoubtedly faced bullying himself. He may have been trying to divert attention to me to take the heat off himself; he may have been parroting the racist attitude of an adult in his life; or he may have just felt like being an asshole that morning. Whichever it was, we got into a bit of a scuffle.

Of course, now I wish I'd handled the situation differently. This was a person so ignorant of Indigenous life that he couldn't draw a distinction between Ojibwe and Mohawk—a distinction Ojibwes and Mohawks themselves are quick to make. After all, there's a few millennia of history there. Sure, he was asking for a punch, but what he needed was to be educated.

When it came to Indigenous history and Indigenous life, that knowledge was in short supply in the Canadian curricula of the eighties and nineties—even in a self-described scholastic bastion like Crescent. We learned more about the treaties signed in Europe than we did about the treaties between the Crown colonizers and the Indigenous people who live on this soil. My only chance to academically engage in a meaningful way with my own history was a single essay I wrote for social studies in my last year titled "Home on Native Land." It was my feeble attempt to outline treaty history in Canada and the current state of land claims—clearly a topic a twelfth grader could encapsulate in a ten-page paper. With so little background and the news blaring headlines about "illegal" blockades and a dead police officer, how much could I really fault my classmate for his ignorance and insensitivity?

As the Oka Crisis unfolded, I learned that there was no escape. To the non-Indigenous world we were all the same: invisible in our suffering, and criminal if we tried to resist it. Crescent couldn't teach me much about who I was as an Indigenous person, but it certainly helped reveal the gaps, and how I could come to grips with them.

In the final year of high school, Crescent organized campus visits to out-of-town universities where many of my classmates would end up: Queen's, Waterloo, Guelph, Wilfrid Laurier, and Western. My chief memory of these visits was the stark whiteness of the students. Some campuses seemed almost completely devoid of people of colour, at least when we visited. I found this utterly terrifying.

In making university a reality for me, private school had fulfilled the implied promise in its sales pitch to my parents. I was thankful for the possibilities that opened up, and grateful to the teachers who'd helped get me there. But I was also determined to escape the culture that existed at Crescent. While many of my classmates made plans to go off to school together, I had no such desire. I wanted something new.

Because, frankly, Crescent had already taught me how to fit into the circles of rich white people, how to move comfortably in a world of pure entitlement. Private school is an entitlement incubator. Everyone has paid to get in, and some parents have made additional donations to the school. As a result, parents feel they can demand more from the school's administrators and teachers, who in turn tend to feel beholden to the people paying for everything. The students mostly reflect this dynamic as well, though their sense of entitlement certainly isn't restricted to school grounds, perhaps because it's something whiteness constantly reinforces. One of the reasons whiteness is so alluring, after all, is that built-in sense of entitlement. And why should that not be its default attitude? When you've murdered and stolen so that you can be centred in everything, you're going to feel authorized to watch the whole world revolve around you. And when your great-grandchildren have never known anything but their comfortable place at the centre of things, they'll willingly overlook the oppression of others that's necessary to keep it.

I had plenty of proximity to whiteness, but it was my brownness that the world typically saw—that it taunted and cast as a threat. However, with my classmates as my expert guides, I learned that half the battle in being entitled is simply behaving that way, given that much of the power of entitlement lies in its performance. Crescent taught me to dream big and to feel licensed in seeing those dreams realized; it prepared me to walk into a room of powerful people and feel worthy of being there. That hasn't helped me much on a personal level. I believe that none of us are truly entitled to anything beyond our own human dignity, and I'd like to keep in check any voice that tries to tell me different.

I have, however, found that entitlement can be incredibly useful in social justice work. When I ask for supports for Indigenous peoples, I don't simply feel warranted in making the request, I feel warranted in getting what I've asked for. I think that's a rare thing in our communities. When Indigenous people ask that the treaties our ancestors signed be honoured or ask to be treated like humans, they're labelled as "entitled." Yet in my experience, Indigenous philosophies and ways of knowing leave no room for entitlement. When you live in constant connection with everything around you, one side feeling entitled will unbalance the relationship and cause it to fail—just look at what colonial entitlement has done to the relationship between Canada and Indigenous peoples.

The entitlement I learned at Crescent is part of the reason I feel custom built to do the work I'm now doing. I know where this country's politicians and power brokers come from. I've gone to school with their children. I've seen how they behave when they think no one's watching. I'm unintimidated and unimpressed. In that way, maybe I'm still a nuisance—just not so little.

CHAPTER 7

Ojibwe Enough

Early in 1992—as the Toronto Blue Jays headed into spring training for what would be their first championship season and I entered my final semester at Crescent—I applied and was accepted to the cinema studies program at the University of Toronto. Years of spending every spare cent I could lay my hands on at the theatre or video store had done little to satisfy my hunger for movies, and even the entrails incident in Tal Zimerman's kitchen hadn't dimmed my desire to make one of my own. There were college programs that taught the technical aspects of film and TV production, but I felt that before I could dive into that world I had to better understand the theory behind it. U of T was one of the few universities in Canada offering a degree in cinema studies back then. Add in the appeal of living on my own in the city and of a campus blessedly far from a monoculture—along with my determination to stay close to the girl I was dating at the time—and the decision was a no-brainer. (Perhaps predictably, the girl and I parted ways early on in my first year.)

But before I could properly enroll, I had to figure out how I was going to pay for it. Money from my dad's family had helped put me through Montcrest and Crescent, but my parents weren't themselves rich. Both in middle management at their respective companies at that point, they couldn't comfortably foot the bill for my tuition and housing—and I certainly hadn't saved up enough from my summer job at Scepter/Ipex, where my dad worked. I'd logged enough time there—mostly in the factory and warehouse, although I'd also spent time as a receptionist and a sales catalogue assembler—to witness firsthand how hard my father worked for his paycheque. While putting in full-time hours he'd attended night school so that he could get a better job within the company, and although I hadn't known it at the time, when Maggie and I were young he'd go back to work after we went to bed, putting in yet more hours while we dreamed the night away. My parents had done enough for me as it was, and I couldn't ask them to do more.

So I looked into a few options for student loans and met with a guidance counsellor at Crescent to discuss potential scholarships and bursaries. Eventually, however, my course was determined by a couple of conversations with my parents—though "conversations" is a bit of a misnomer, as they did all the talking; and "they" isn't correct either, as the driving force and deciding voice came entirely from my mom.

At the time, if you were a First Nations kid you could apply to have your post-secondary education paid for through the community. The government of Canada provided funding to a body then called the National Aboriginal Achievement Foundation (NAAF), which distributed it through scholarships to First Nations, Métis, and Inuit youth. Nowadays, the NAAF (renamed Indspire in 2012) is oversubscribed and doesn't have enough money to meet the demand, so there's a gap between the number of students applying for funds and the number of students who actually receive them. Back then, though, the NAAF had money because, sadly, so few Indigenous youth attended university. If I applied, I was basically guaranteed to get what I needed. The big talks with my parents were about whether I should apply at all. And those conversations revealed a conflict in my identity that I've struggled with for much of my life.

When I eventually did start going to U of T (spoiler, I know), the university had just opened something called First Nations House, a resource centre and gathering place for Indigenous students. By that point in my life I was eager to form my own connections with the community—ones not necessarily defined by family ties—and to discover my particular place within it. First Nations House seemed like a good place to start. I dropped in a few times, but I always felt uncomfortable there, as though I didn't belong. Most of the other students had grown up in First Nations communities; they weren't from the city. I remember that, during one of my visits, there was a drum circle. I didn't know how to drum or sing or speak my language or do anything, it seemed to me. Everyone was welcoming, and in retrospect I should've spent more time there, but I couldn't get over my own embarrassment and shame. I couldn't shake the feeling that, although I was Ojibwe and deeply proud of my heritage, I wasn't Ojibwe *enough*.

Every time we'd arrive for a visit at Serpent River I'd have the same feeling—there, though, being surrounded by relatives would drive it away. I know that my insecurities trace back to things forcibly taken from my family, first in the years my grandmother spent at residential school and afterward as she sought to make sense of herself and her life in the wake of that trauma, yet it's still hard not to feel them as personal failings. Even today, when I'm more connected to the broader Indigenous community than at any other time in my life, it still comes over me from time to time—self-consciousness and shame in not knowing my language, in not having grown up on the reserve and as part of the community. Knowing on an intellectual level that none of that is my fault, or my mother's, grandmother's, or great-grandparents', that it's a desired outcome of centuries of colonialism, doesn't make the pain and confusion much easier to bear. But it is worth writing here.

Attacking Indigenous identity has been central to colonial success since small groups of traders gave way to large boatloads of settlers. For colonialism's avaricious pursuit of wealth and reckless exploitation of natural resources to be anything but a crime, for the nation states those forces created to be anything but illegitimate, there had to be nothing here before them. To acknowledge Indigenous nations and Indigenous humanity in a meaningful way would be to acknowledge the atrocities committed against them. Unwilling to face that truth, colonial states must not only erase or obscure that history; they must also try to force these nations—nations that have existed for thousands of years—to question and squabble over their own identities. And at an individual level, colonial states need Indigenous peoples to either assimilate completely or assimilate enough to be ostracized by their own communities and families. Anything less is a potential threat.

This is why policing First Nations, Métis, and Inuit identity was a key part of the Indian Act. Granting the state its own powers to decide who is Indigenous and who is not allowed the state to constantly move the goalposts of Indigeneity. Colonial states want Indigenous people to be unsure of their own identities, of the identities of their neighbours, and of the identities of their leaders. It was and is a way to separate communities from the land and each other. Indigenous people being too ashamed or confused to participate in Indigenous ceremony is colonialism winning. And within that confusion, they want non-Indigenous peoples to be able to adopt Indigenous identities. What is colonialism but the theft of identity so that others may wear it?

The Indian Act is among Canada's oldest laws, and almost certainly one of its most important, but when I was a kid it wasn't taught in school. My knowledge of it came—at least, at first—from living under it. All Canadians live under the Indian Act, but of course, only Indians actually have to pay much attention to it.

There are plenty of books about the Act and the harm it has done, and in some ways, this is another. If you're looking for a truly comprehensive critique, though, Bob Joseph's *21 Things You May Not Know About the Indian Act* does an excellent job breaking everything down. You should read it.

For our purposes, the easiest way to describe the Indian Act is that it's the law dictating the relationship between First Nations and Canada as a state. (Although Métis and Inuit are considered Indians in most practical senses, they don't fall under the Indian Act.) The key elements of the relationship governed by the Act are the reserve system, the band offices or governments meant to oversee and administer the reserves, and status.

So what you have is a colonial settler state creating a law that dictates where an ethnic minority can live, how their local governments will work, and who is eligible for citizenship in the first place. Not exactly how one sovereign nation treats other sovereign nations, is it?

In its creation and enforcement of reserves and band councils, the Indian Act is an overt attack on First Nations' sovereignty. Its rules about so-called "status" attack Indigenous identity itself.

The word actually reveals the intent. "Status" is something to be sought, but also something that is not achievable for all. In this case, status is recorded on a registry, which certifies that, under the Indian Act, an individual is recognized as being an Indian. That person is then assigned a unique number; but that's not all: it comes with a card!

Since its inception, the process of designating official status has been central to the government's ability to systematically reduce the number of Indigenous people who can hold treaty rights. This, of course, furthers the ultimate goal: the elimination of the Indian problem. If there ever comes a day under the Indian Act when there are no more status Indians, well, then there's no more need for the Act, for treaties, or for anything else to govern the "relationship." With no one left to challenge its sovereignty, Canada will have completed its colonial mission.

As a young kid whose sense of self was still evolving, I actually took comfort in that first wallet-sized, red and beige status card. It was proof of something, I thought, even if that something was only that the government deemed me Indian enough to make it official. It also made me unusual, at least for East York. After all, none of my friends had status cards. Of course, I'd never needed a status card for others to label me an Indian—at least not in the city. But the card *was* somehow reassuring. It made my identity tangible in a sense, something I could take out of my wallet.

It didn't take long for the shine to fade, though, as I soon learned about the inequities built into the determination of status. My sister and I were eligible for status only because our grandmother Norma never actually married our grandfather Jack. Until the Indian Act was amended in 1985, when a First Nations woman with status married someone without, she and her children lost their status. (This wasn't true for First Nations men who married someone without status.) Thus some of my cousins, whose grandparents did marry, weren't eligible. Such arbitrary exclusions created divisions within communities where there hadn't been any, again to the advantage of the colonizer. And even though the 1985 amendment allowed many of those who'd lost their status to regain it, gender discrimination around status wasn't entirely abolished until recently, and only after years of advocacy by Indigenous women.

Once you have it, status does come with treaty rights, so among other things, if you show the card in Ontario stores, they won't charge you some of the sales tax. That's in theory, though. In practice, this is often a challenging, even humiliating moment. Many retailers aren't experienced with the cards, so it can be a rigmarole just to save a few dollars. What's worse is the reaction of other customers, which can range from bewilderment to resentment to outright racism. I've gone long stretches where I just didn't bother; it wasn't worth the potential hassle.

Status being represented by a laminated card also means that it can be faked and co-opted. The last few years have seen a noticeable increase in non-Indigenous people posing as Indigenous people, usually with fake status cards. Métis identity is claimed most frequently, although typically it's not actually Métis but rather an aggregation of mixed heritages often dependent on a sole Indigenous ancestor who existed centuries ago. It's not unusual for this claimed ancestor to not even be Indigenous; many of these imposters claim the same relative. Scholar Darryl Leroux has written an excellent book on the subject, *Distorted Descent: White Claims to Indigenous Identity*, which looks at claims of "Eastern Métis" identity in places like the Maritimes, where there never were any Métis. These false claims may seem innocuous if you consider only the sales tax, but they've been used to oppose the land claims and territorial agreements of legitimate Indigenous people and to take career and educational opportunities meant for First Nations, Métis, and Inuit, further marginalizing us and challenging our self-determination.

Allowing settlers to claim Indigenous identity is a key tactic of colonial states. It facilitates the erasure necessary so that settler claims to nationhood can appear legitimate. It's also central to the mythology of colonialism. Rooted in white supremacy, this mythology tells us that settlers are superior because they adapt so easily to a new land and its cultures and customs that they dominate them. In turn, it paints Indigenous cultures and nations as simplistic, as nothing close to the complex systems and cultures of colonial powers, as lacking in governance, economies, and established social orders. Indigenous identity becomes something easily described and capable of being distilled into a single laminated card.

Under this constant assault from outside forces, it's no wonder issues of identity are front and centre for many nations. These days, false claims of Indigenous identity are often attempts to occupy the space and opportunities that may be afforded an Indigenous person. The irony should be lost on no one, given that not long ago many of our relations felt they had to disguise *their* identities in hope of a brighter future. But the tactic itself is an extension of the same bag of tricks colonialism has always employed.

These are complex and emotional issues to address, especially on the personal level, but it's necessary to confront them. Like many, I fear a reliance on colonial measures of identity and nationhood, as they were never created to include First Nations' perspectives. I also worry that the recent reliance on self-identification—allowing people to claim their own Indigeneity—has led to false or misinformed claims, which complicate the sovereignty work so many others are engaging in.

I recently renewed my status card. I'd had the same one my whole life, with the same thirty-year-old black-and-white photo taken at a mall in east Toronto. When I first got it, there was no expiry date. It was something we joked about—that you never expired from being an Indian. That didn't mean I was exempt from the ravages of time, however. Increasingly, whenever I'd pull it out at a store the cashier would look at it, look at me, and then look at it again. I guess the years were starting to catch up.

My chance to update the photo came on a family trip to Serpent River. We were there to honour my Auntie Mina, Norma's youngest sister, who was to be buried in the community graveyard where generations of our family reside. It's a small cemetery, surrounded by trees, that sits off the highway, next to the community centre. On the day of the burial we entered through a small gate with high grass on either side and walked among the gravestones, some just old crosses, the names long rubbed away by the wind and rain. So many Meawasiges, the same names that hang on the genealogy chart in the trading post. So much history.

That night we had a feast in Mina's honour in the community centre's big double gym. It had been a decade since the last family gathering of that size. There were uncles and cousins galore, people I hadn't seen in years. Over the course of the night, each table was introduced and everyone at it explained their connection to Mina. She was the person who'd always brought our family together. Even sick in the hospital, she joked that she was doing it again—making everyone come to see her.

Mina was the last matriarch of that generation of our family. I loved her deeply. She had the same quick, easy sense of humour as my grandmother, and the sound of their laughter echoes in my brain as pure pleasure and happiness. Like Norma, Mina was a terrific card player. She was always up for a game of crib, and took no prisoners at euchre. Like my grandmother, she was physically small but occupied an enormous place in our hearts. Her passing was felt across our family, and it was only fitting that we would gather once more.

Earlier in the day we'd stopped by the band office to have lunch. While we were eating I decided to see if I could get my status card renewed. I walked over to the office. There were two cheerful women inside.

"How can we help you?" one of them asked as I entered.

"I was wondering if I could get my status card renewed," I said, half statement, half question.

"Sure, Jesse, no problem. We'll have to go take a picture in the other office," came the answer. "Hey, any new movies we should see?"

In that moment, if there wasn't a smile on my face, there was one in my heart. Here I was, standing in my community's band office for the first time in years, and the ladies there not only knew who I was without ever looking at my card but they even asked me for movie recommendations. I could both hardly believe it and completely believe it. This is my community. These are my people. Not because of some card the government gives me, but because they claim me.

These days I shudder to think I could ever have found any comfort in that card, but I did find enormous comfort and joy in that office. The new laminated card had a colour photo of me and an expiry date. Even before it was handed over I felt I'd gotten what I'd come for. I told the two women about a couple of movies they could find on Netflix. Then I went back to lunch, feeling that I'd been healed.

So many of the conflicts I may have held inside were resolved on that trip. My family felt so embraced by our community, by our extended family, that when it came time to leave it was Serpent River that felt like home. That's community. Not some fucking card.

I hadn't visited Serpent River in a while when it was time to go to university. Life had just been too busy. As my parents and I discussed whether I should apply for the NAAF funding, the confusion and conflict that surrounds every Indigenous identity was what we were really being forced to consider and contend with. There was no question that I met all the official criteria, but there *was* a built-in sense that, were I to apply, some people in Serpent River would potentially take issue. They might object on the grounds that I lived in the city, that I hadn't grown up on the rez or faced the conditions and challenges that too often come with life in a First Nations community.

Now, whether anyone in Serpent River actually felt this way, I don't know. But to me those hypothetical criticisms were legitimate enough to at least warrant some real thought. My proximity to whiteness, meaning its presence in my family, allowed for much of the not-inconsiderable privilege I'd accessed in my life. I thought it only fair to hold myself to account and properly question whether I was the "type" of Indigenous student the scholarships were intended to help.

My mom, though, was having none of it.

As we discussed whether to, as she put it, "have this government fund pay," my mom was extremely clear in her convictions. She listened to my concerns, and acknowledged that there might be people in Serpent River who saw me as undeserving, but when I was done, she put her foot down: "Jesse, they've taken so much from our family," she told me. "You are going to take this."

I think it was the first time we'd ever talked about the personal impact of colonialism on our family. That's not to say, though, that there hadn't been hints about the way my mom understood our history. My grandmother was a devout Catholic; my mom was not. She barely concealed her disdain for the Church, proudly noting that although she and my father were married in a church, they'd lied to the priest in order to make it happen. It wasn't long after my grandmother told me about her experience at residential school that I realized my mom's dislike of Catholicism stemmed from her knowledge of what it had done to our family and the role it had played in the theft of our land, language, and culture. All that effort and evil just to hold sway over a family for a couple of generations. It would almost be funny if it weren't so heartbreaking.

It wasn't that I'd ever been discouraged from investigating the injustices my family had endured; it was just that it had never gone beyond that one conversation with my grandmother in the kitchen. The crimes themselves are, of course, a key part of the reason for that silence. My mother and her siblings didn't experience the horror of residential schools firsthand, but they were raised by someone who did. Like me, they grew up in Toronto largely divorced from the community, and yet they were situated much closer to the core of that trauma than I was. Having been forcibly removed from her family by the state, my grandmother's ability to build and maintain family relationships had been damaged. She could be emotionally distant with her children, and had difficulty creating for them a real sense of warmth and security—those same feelings of "home" she herself had been denied by her time at St. Joseph's.

The damage wrought by residential schools has been passed down in various forms throughout my family. It's an unwanted inheritance that has played out in broken relationships and addiction issues decades after the initial traumas. Of course, similar pains, setbacks, and struggles exist on my dad's side of the family. But they lack a history of state interference; their crises are devoid of the political meaning that infuses the same issues on the Ojibwe side. You don't get the sense looking at my dad's family that there were greater forces dictating outcomes. One of the key differences between the Wentes and the Meawasiges is agency.

Today, many members of my family have made huge progress rebuilding the relationships residential schools destroyed. My mom is deeply tied to the Indigenous community through volunteer work; my Aunt Bonnie gave up a successful career on Bay Street to become an artist and developed the Indigenous Visual Culture program at the Ontario College of Art and Design; and my Uncle Rob charges to the front lines of Indigenous protest movements, sending me dispatches and footage from the blockades at Tyendinaga. In short, I have ample models in my family for my own activist work today, but it took time for them to rediscover their identities and forge those connections to the Indigenous community. They simply weren't that engaged or political when I was young, and Serpent River itself was healing, holding a powwow again in 1990 for the first time in many years.

So by the time I was planning for university, my mom was pulling no punches. "This money is a small part of what's owed to our family," she said that day. "Don't let anyone ever tell you that you aren't owed it. You are absolutely owed it and way, way more for what happened. You're going to take this money, and you're going to go to the university you want."

She was, however, quick to add the caveat that being owed the money didn't mean I'd be relieved of obligation if I actually received it. The NAAF did eventually pay for my tuition and rent and provided me with a stipend. But before I saw a penny, before I'd even applied, my mom made it clear that taking the money came with a responsibility unlike any I'd known—a sacred obligation.

"There will come a time," she said, "when you know in your heart you have to turn back to your community."

To my mother, accepting help from the NAAF created a commitment to pay back the debt, not with money but instead with love, effort, time, advocacy, art—whatever my particular combination of talent, achievement, and experience would prepare me to offer. She was certain that one day the knowledge of how I could help my community would strike me, that my life would build to that moment of clarity.

"When that happens you have to use everything you've got to help," she added.

That moment did come, exactly as she said it would.

Mom, you led by example. You gave back everything you learned, everything you were given, and more. I am trying to do the same.

PART II

The Story I Told Myself

CHAPTER 8

"Do You Know This Guy?"

Shortly after I finished at Crescent, my Grandpa Tom turned up with a graduation present. It wasn't going to top my classmates' for ostentation—one of them had been given an entire brewery to mark the occasion—but Tom's present meant the world to me. Beaming as he showed off the giant Panasonic television he'd bought me, he said simply, "If you're going to watch movies, you're going to need a good TV."

The thing had to weigh at least two hundred pounds. Lugging it up the stairs to the studio apartment I'd rented above an egg shop in Kensington Market nearly killed me. And once I'd gotten it through the door I barely had any apartment left; that giant Panasonic filled the room. It was a fantastic TV, though; it had very good blacks. And my grandfather was right: I was definitely going to be watching movies.

It wasn't quite up to the thousand-plus movies a year I would eventually watch as a professional critic, but studying film at U of T allowed me to indulge my passion. It also offered me the chance to write about film with a political read. My mom's informal questioning had prepared me.

I wrote about representation in blaxploitation films. I wrote about *Alien*'s Ellen Ripley through the lens of feminist theory. But I never tackled Indigenous representation.

In my defence, I was mostly out of luck in the classroom, given how little Indigenous cinema was being made or discussed. But my years in university did inform my understanding of Indigenous identity in other ways. I was out from under my parents' roof and living on my own in the city for the first time. Those facts alone seemed to increase my exposure to the police, and the lessons they taught were unforgettable.

In my first year I still wore my hair buzzed, the way I had in high school, although by that time it was less an act of rebellion than one of practicality. I couldn't afford the barber anymore, so I bought my own trimmer and shaved my head once a week or so. Yes, this financially prudent fashion choice meant I was the bald guy in class. And yes, my bald head wasn't the most attractive bald head out there. But it was easy, cheap, and occasionally therapeutic. It also had the effect of keeping people away, which, though unintentional, was welcome given how shy I still was at that point.

I met my future wife, Julie, when I was sporting the bald head. She later told me that my look scared her a little bit at first, which might partly explain why she was so encouraging when I decided to let my hair grow out. I'd never had long hair—it had been forbidden at the private schools I attended, after all—and it took months of care to achieve it, since I was starting from bare earth. Eventually, though, it hung dark and long, almost all the way to my backside.

For an Indigenous person, long hair is always freighted with meaning. It's a visible connection to traditional ways and beliefs, and an equally visible threat to colonial culture and its systems and structures. When I started wearing my hair long, I was actively distancing myself from whiteness—my own and that of the culture at large. My hair instantly marked me as Indigenous, and I found that ever-present signal of my pride in who I was and where I came from deeply affirming.

There was a flipside to being so visible, though. And it didn't help that my personal and follicular growth roughly coincided with the release of *Dances with Wolves*. The film, which won the Academy Award for Best Picture in 1991 and which I instantly disliked, was immensely popular and fuelled a brief mainstream fascination with Indigeneity. This fleeting popularity had some positive effects, including a small drip of inclusion in the film business. Some major works, like *Once Were Warriors* and, later, *Smoke Signals*, found global audiences, and impressive figures like Tantoo Cardinal, Shirley Cheechoo, Alanis Obomsawin, and the Podemski sisters began to expand their influence and activity. But mostly the fascination was focused on commodifying Indigenous art, fashion, and people for the benefit of a white consumer. The 1990s would see only marginal movement for Indigenous rights and well-being; that decade would instead be defined by the confrontation in Kanehsatake, the Ipperwash Crisis, and the murder of Dudley George by the Ontario Provincial Police. As always seems to be the case, we were useful as objects, as pop culture artifacts, but not as people. Our humanity only got in the way of the desire for our aesthetic.

My long hair was a magnet for white attention in a way my person-hood never was. Strangers rarely approached to ask after my thoughts and feelings, but they felt comfortable asking to touch my hair or surreptitiously snapping a photo of me. In one oddly memorable incident a year or two after university, Julie and I were eating breakfast and reading the paper at a diner when we noticed a large family of German tourists at the next table delightedly whispering and pointing at me. For those who don't know, Germany has a small obsession with Indigenous people, to the degree that there exists a robust niche travel market in Germans coming to Canada to experience "real Indigenous culture." Seeing an Indian, live and in the flesh, before their eggs arrived had made this family's day. I doubt they would've given me a second look if I'd still had my bald head. Germany has no First Nations, Métis, or Inuit.

Their image of what an Indian looks like was created in and imported from Hollywood—and their "Indian" definitely has long hair.

Other interactions were considerably more perilous and degrading. I was constantly followed by suspicious shopkeepers and security guards, who seemed to assume I was there to steal. I was shouted at on the street. "*Maudit autochtone écoeurant*," yelled one racist heckler as we walked down the street in Montreal. Julie had to tell me that it meant "disgusting damned native."

By far the most unwelcome and unsettling bit of attention, however, was the increased scrutiny that came from the police.

In university, I suffered from insomnia. Instead of lying in bed fretting, I'd get up and putter around the apartment or, more often, go out for a walk. I'd wander the market for a while and then head all the way to Yonge Street and spend some time in the arcades. I quickly got used to the fact that these walks could be interrupted by an interaction with the police.

"Hey, you there!"

These were not quiet parts of town, even in the middle of the night. There were always plenty of people around, and yet almost instinctively I knew it was me they wanted. And it was. They'd stop me and demand to know who I was, where I was going, what I was doing out at night. Sometimes they'd ask for ID, other times they'd stay in the cruiser, questioning me through the window.

It took me a while to realize that their interest had a lot to do with my being Indigenous. I'd been raised to respect police officers and to believe that they didn't take people to task for no reason. *You must have done something. Why else would they be bothering you?* This would run through my head even when I knew I'd done nothing wrong.

I'd started smoking pot in university, which didn't hasten my understanding. It sometimes helped with my insomnia, so I was often high on my walks across Dundas Street, meaning that when I was stopped then a part of me felt, "Oh, I *have* done something wrong; that must be why." This despite the fact that the stops didn't usually involve a search, and that the cops had no way of knowing I was stoned before questioning me.

Pot wasn't the only explanation, or excuse, I reached for. "Well, you know, I'm young, so it's maybe because I'm a teenager or a twenty-something and I look threatening," I'd tell myself. "I'm a big dude, so maybe that's just scary."

Just as I had that day at Topham Park, I piled up excuses, trying to find a legitimate reason for the stops. I didn't want to think they were simply for who I was. Because then I'd be screwed—and there was no resolving that. By the six or seventh time, though, it clicked and I had to force myself to address it: *Right, I get it now. It's not that I'm stoned or young or big, and it's not a coincidence. It's that I'm an Indian.*

Now, in my mid-forties, I've been profiled so many times and in so many ways that it just doesn't have the effect it used to. The fear and vulnerability have been drained out of me, replaced by weariness and, occasionally, anger. When I think back on that initial realization, though, I remember how unnerving it was—how terrifying, really. As a kid, I wouldn't necessarily have understood what was at play when I was being othered. But as my understanding deepened and I could comprehend the danger more fully, the same ignorance and prejudice I'd felt at moments in my childhood took on a new level of menace when embodied by the police.

I was always able to maintain my composure when talking to an officer, but when they'd finally drive off I'd find myself shaking uncontrollably—from anger, fear, or raw adrenalin I'm not sure. Eventually, I had to consider whether the risk of these encounters was worth the relief of a walk and some fun in an arcade. I decided it was, and I kept walking.

The stops continued even as, shortly after university, I was invited to sit on the Toronto Police Chief's Youth Advisory Committee. This was a group of young people, most of whom were racialized, who regularly met with then chief of police, David Boothby. The discussion tended to centre on how best to convince more racialized youths to join the police force, but we also took on broader issues, like the department's uneasy relationships with racialized communities. It was, in theory, the perfect venue in which to raise concerns about the way the city's police treated Indigenous youth. But it was also the first time I'd ever participated in anything like the committee, and I was uncomfortable speaking up about my experiences. I never brought up the police stops—something I deeply regret now.

There are reasons beyond shyness for my silence back then. For one thing, I was sure nothing would be done even if I did speak out. This was, after all, the leader of the same police force that had been harassing me for years. For another, I was worried about my fledgling career at the CBC somehow being damaged if I drew attention to myself. Mostly, though, I was just embarrassed: embarrassed to be someone who attracted so much suspicion, even though I'd done nothing wrong. I thought the whole thing was better hidden. So I hid it—from the committee, from my coworkers at the CBC, from my parents and friends, and from Julie. But, as it turned out, I could only do that for so long.

It was before Julie and I moved in together. I was walking her home one night, sometime around eleven, after an evening out. I was wearing jeans and a hoodie, nothing special. She looked lovely as always, dressed in a dark blue dress with flowers and buttons down the front, black shorts underneath because the dress would flare up in the breeze. Her favourite Doc Martens boots on her feet. We were holding hands, as lovers do.

The cruiser approached from behind. I didn't notice it until it pulled up right beside us; two officers got out. I should've been worried about what was about to happen to me, but all I could think about was Julie. I hoped she wasn't scared.

They never spoke to me. I heard one of them start talking to Julie, as I stood there worried about what might happen.

"Are you okay?" he asked, his voice a model of official concern.

"Yes," she responded.

"Do you know this guy?"

"Yes, he's my boyfriend."

"Where are you going?"

"He's walking me home," she said, a note of anger creeping into her voice. "Did we do anything?"

The officer continued to question her for what felt like a couple of minutes. His partner just stood behind me waiting for the interview with Julie to finish. Neither asked me anything the entire time. They barely even acknowledged my presence. I was an object—a threatening part of the scenery. Eventually, they got back in the cruiser and left.

Julie looked over at me to make sure I was okay. She took my face in her hands. She was pissed off and shaken up. She wanted to do something, *anything*, about what had just happened—to erase it or make it right.

I just shrugged. I told her it was no big deal, that it happened sometimes. Maybe it was because I was young, or big. Maybe I'd looked threatening. I told her we should just put it behind us. I tried to act unfazed.

Inside I felt embarrassed and upset. Humiliated in front of my girlfriend. Emasculated. Powerless. We were pretty quiet the rest of the way to her place, both tied up in our own thoughts. I dropped her off and went home, and at some point between then and now, I realized how lucky I was.

My night had ended seeing off my beautiful girlfriend and heading home to sleep in my own bed. Rodney Naistus hadn't been so lucky; Lawrence Wegner and Neil Stonechild hadn't been so lucky. All three of these Indigenous men had interactions with the police that may not have started out much differently from mine. All three had frozen to death on the outskirts of town, left there after being dropped off by the police. I lived by the mantra *Stay out of the back of the cruiser*. Ultimately, though, it wasn't really a choice; it was just something that happened to you—like an illness. I was lucky. I'd gotten off easy.

Chantel Moore was killed by police in Edmundston, New Brunswick, on June 4, 2020. Moore was twenty-six years old and a member of Tla-o-qui-aht First Nation. She was shot when an Edmundston officer arrived at her apartment to perform a "wellness check." According to police reports, Moore wielded a knife. The incident is now being investigated by the Bureau des Enquêtes Indépendantes (BEI), Quebec's independent police watchdog, since New Brunswick doesn't have its own police oversight body. Moore's estate has filed suit.

Eight days later, on June 12, Rodney Levi, a member of Metepenagiag Mi'kmaq Nation, was killed by the New Brunswick RCMP after they were called to a home Levi was visiting. The owner of the home, Reverend Brodie MacLeod, would later release a statement describing Levi as "a welcomed guest" of his family. The BEI is also investigating Levi's death.

The deaths of Moore and Levi came at a time when, owing to police violence, North America already felt like a tinderbox.

Just three months earlier, Breonna Taylor, a twenty-six-year-old Black woman, had been shot in her own bed by police in Louisville, Kentucky, during a raid on her home. As of this writing, the officers responsible will not be charged.

A month after Taylor's death, in Winnipeg, three Indigenous people—Eishia Hudson, sixteen; Stewart Kevin Andrews, twenty-two; and Jason Collins, thirty-six—died in police-involved incidents in the span of ten days. Manitoba's Independent Investigative Unit is investigating all three cases.

Then in May, a Black man named George Floyd was killed when Minneapolis police officer Derek Chauvin knelt on his neck for eight minutes and forty-six seconds. Unlike the other killings listed here, Floyd's was captured on video. As he was held face down, being suffocated, Floyd repeatedly said he couldn't breathe; he called out for his mother. Chauvin has been charged, as have three other officers who were present at the scene.

Meanwhile, back in Canada, in June 2020 Rodney Levi became the sixth Indigenous person to die in a police-related incident in a span of less than two and a half months. At the time, that total exceeded the number of Indigenous people who'd died from COVID-19, which reached Canada in late February.

There was, of course, also no shortage of non-lethal police violence against Indigenous people around the same period. The day before Levi was killed, video surfaced of the March 10 arrest of Athabasca Chipewyan First Nations Chief Allan Adam by the Wood Buffalo RCMP at a casino in Fort McMurray, Alberta. The footage shows an officer tackling Adam, striking him in the head, and putting him in a chokehold. The incident is being investigated by the Alberta Serious Incident Response Team.

Although videos of police brutality like the violence visited on Adam have been disturbingly if predictably common since the LAPD's assault of Rodney King was filmed back in 1991, the experience of watching Floyd's murder, viewed in the midst of a pandemic, seemed a last straw for many. Protests began almost immediately, led by the Black Lives Matter movement, the most public manifestation of an urgent push to defund the police in the wake of ongoing violence against Black and Brown people.

Those protests quickly extended to Canada, where Indigenous people joined in the calls to take meaningful action against systemic racism and state-sanctioned racial violence. And it's no wonder our voices have been crucial in this movement, as the sheer amount of violence experienced by Indigenous people at the hands of police may exceed our grimmest expectations. According to a database created by the CBC to track fatal encounters where police force was used, Indigenous people account for 16 percent of those deaths over the past twenty years, despite comprising only 4.21 percent of the population. Black people are overrepresented as well, making up 8.63 percent of those deaths while accounting for only 2.92 percent of the population. Also of note: every single Indigenous person killed during this period was suffering from either mental health or addiction issues—at least according to police reports and court records.

That Indigenous and Black people are overrepresented among victims of lethal police violence should come as no surprise. We know from the overwhelming evidence that there is a disproportionate, racist application of police violence. But we must also acknowledge the underpinnings of those violent institutions. Policing, as devised, constructed, and utilized by settler-colonial nations, has always been about controlling Indigenous and Black communities.

The North-West Mounted Police force, formed in 1873 by John A. Macdonald, Canada's first prime minister, was modelled after the Royal Irish Constabulary, a paramilitary force used to assert British control over Ireland. Canada had only recently completed "purchase" of its territory from the Hudson's Bay Company. Thus, the original mandate of the Mounties was to secure Canadian sovereignty in the west, which at the time included much of what is now Northern Quebec and Ontario, extending through Manitoba, Saskatchewan, and Alberta and into the Northwest Territories. Those lands were, of course, populated by a majority of First Nations, Métis, and Inuit.

It's similar to the brutal origin of policing in America, which has its roots in the slave-catching units of the antebellum South. In both countries, the primary function of the police was to assert and maintain colonial sovereignty and to protect private property. Slaves were considered property, as was the land from which Indigenous peoples were removed.

It was the Mounties who carried out the forced relocation of First Nations and Métis to reserves, and who were responsible for keeping them there. Those who wouldn't go were denied food and supplies until they had no choice but to comply.

It was the Mounties who would come to our homes to take our children to residential schools.

And today, when Indigenous people publicly resist colonialism, it is the Mounties who arrive—in militarized vehicles instead of on horseback, but still armed to the teeth. In 2019 in Wet'suwet'en, an unceded territory in what is currently called British Columbia, the RCMP was brought in to confront the Indigenous nation asserting its sovereignty over its territory in the face of an unwanted oil pipeline. And across the United States in 2020, police and paramilitary forces were repeatedly deployed to protests—not to prevent violence against people, but rather to protect buildings and other property. Indeed, whether protests take place on sovereign Indigenous land or in urban centres, it's when police arrive that things turn violent. That's actually the point.

So, the history and origin of policing in Canada is based in racism and white supremacy. It's also inextricably linked to the denial of Indigenous people's rights and sovereignty. This remains fundamentally true today. Numerous reports, including those produced by the Truth and Reconciliation Commission and the National Inquiry into Missing and Murdered Indigenous Women and Girls, have called for substantial reform of the RCMP, if not the outright elimination of the force. And in a report released in November 2020, former Supreme Court of Canada justice Michel Bastarache wrote that "a toxic culture prevails in the RCMP," one that "encourages, or at least tolerates, misogynistic, racist, and homophobic attitudes among many members ... The problem is systemic in nature and cannot be corrected solely by punishing a few 'bad apples.'" Bastarache's report came in the wake of the Merlo-Davidson settlement, which saw the federal government pay more than $125,000,000 to claimants who had experienced sexual harassment and gender or sexual orientation–based discrimination while working for the RCMP.

Can police and the wider system of incarceration be reformed, given its roots in colonial efforts to sustain and protect capitalism? I have serious doubts.

Even as the events of summer 2020 firmly embedded the idea of defunding the police into mainstream public discourse, that notion was still largely being met with words. In the case of the City of Toronto, the result was an actual increase in the police budget.

Defunding the police—meaning decreasing departmental budgets in order to reallocate those funds to other social programs capable of replacing some current police duties—is a reasoned response to current police practices. If our governments, at every level, were to invest in systems that address the underlying reasons for crime—namely poverty, addiction, and mental health—the need for police would almost certainly decrease, if not completely disappear.

Reallocating those resources would also keep police from having to respond to situations they are ill-equipped to address or handle responsibly, such as calls when someone is in mental health distress. Why are police performing a "wellness check" on Chantel Moore when there are people far better trained to handle those situations, and who could do so without bringing weaponry? The answer, of course, is because those services either don't exist in Edmundston and elsewhere or are so underfunded as to be unable to take on these duties. Recent studies have found that the police spend most of their response visits dealing with mental health crises and not actual crimes.

For decades, social scientists and others have argued that police and prisons are not effective at preventing crime. The most effective deterrents are economic equality and access to housing and health care. Police don't prevent crime, they respond to it, and even then they don't actually solve much of it. With crimes such as sexual assault and rape, the majority of incidents aren't even reported, let alone resolved.

Police should be the absolute last resort for a society, not its first line of defence. In fact, we should stop viewing police as a defensive or protective force and see it for what it really is: an almost exclusively punitive institution designed mainly to reinforce the status quo and protect property.

As hard as it is for many to imagine, this land has known many alternatives to our current systems of justice. Before colonialism, First Nations had their own structures and practices for dealing with crime. There were no prisons, although there was capital punishment. Some nations used banishment—since being cast out from the community was understood to rank among the most severe of repercussions. Restorative justice was common, although the crimes it addressed, primarily theft, were infrequent, given that the community provided for those in need.

Capitalism brought police to these lands, along with so many other damaging systems and structures, because it required police as a central tool to sustain itself. This is also true of poverty. Capitalism needs poor people so that it can maintain a ready population forced to work for the lowest wages possible. It needs police to protect the wealthy and their property, sure, but also to control the impoverished in a way that avoids any challenge to existing power centres. Police are the shock troops of capitalism, deployed to protect it at all costs, and as we already know, Indigenous and Black lives are never assigned much value in these situations.

What has to be clear by now is that policing as we know it isn't making our societies safer; instead, for many, it makes life so much more dangerous. And given how much we spend on police, at all levels of government, it's shocking how little accountability they're subject to. We pay for policing but have little control over how it operates.

Of course, defunding or abolishing the police won't achieve a more equitable society without other support systems being built up or redesigned to address systemic violence and the underlying issues that lead to crime. Swapping in other existing social programs and "supports" in place of police may not be all that much better in certain cases and for certain communities. For example, in many Black and Indigenous communities, social workers can do as much harm as police. Social workers have been used to remove Indigenous children from their parents, citing child and family safety reasons—an ongoing practice that only furthers the work begun in the residential schools, using the poverty and addiction of its victims against them. Here, reallocating police resources to other broken systems would amount to a diversionary tactic. Treating the root causes of inequality is the only path to lasting solutions, and it's one that requires a vast redistribution of wealth and resources: the exact thing police were created to prevent.

The current iteration of capitalism under which we all operate features wealthy individuals and corporations often paying less in taxes than average households, at least proportionally. The hoarding of wealth is at an all-time high, and there is little space for the class mobility that marked earlier generations. If communities are unable to escape poverty and its associated harms, then the reasons we give to justify the existence of police will remain. If everyone had a basic income and reliable access to housing, health care, education, and child care, then capitalism would, ironically, benefit, with healthier workers and more consumers. What we wouldn't have is the largest disparity of wealth in human history.

We must unlearn the individualism that has conditioned us to believe personal achievement and success to be our society's pinnacle, one that should come with wealth and privilege. The COVID-19 pandemic should have reminded us that we are social animals; that we exist better in relation to each other than on our own; that the success and health of our neighbour contributes to our own health and happiness. It's this vision of society that should underpin all our systems and structures, with community at its centre, not the individual. This is how many Indigenous communities organized themselves. If we recommitted to those models, keeping one another's best interest at the centre of everything we built, how much would we really need police? How much harm could we prevent?

Attracting police attention merely by existing as an Indigenous person made me, sadly, typical. And in changing myself to try to minimize those interactions, I'm also not unique. When I eventually cut my long hair, the decision was based on a number of factors. Taking proper care of it was a pain. *Sure.* I was ready for a change. *Uh-huh.* The real reason, of course, was that I was exhausted by the scrutiny it attracted. I was sick of being followed in stores and yelled at on the street. I was sick of being treated as either a threat or a mythological creature, with little room in between to just be myself. Most of all, though, I was sick of getting stopped and questioned by the police.

A hairstyle is, of course, a minor thing, a detail, nothing to get too fussed about. But when even those tiny things are policed, it becomes nearly impossible to make a comfortable, normal life for yourself. When some tiny and unexpected aspect of the way you look or think or walk or dress is always setting off someone around you, you're left confused, scrambling, and on the defensive. And when the people being set off carry state-sanctioned firearms, it takes real resolve, community support, and a certain degree of mental gymnastics not to live in a constant state of fear.

Years had passed since I'd had anything beyond a small trim, so the prospect of a full haircut was a daunting and even emotionally charged one. Fortunately, some friends recommended a hairdresser, Loretta, who'd worked in the film business. I went to meet her. We talked about what I wanted to do and she made sure I knew I was in good hands. Then, when she began cutting off the hair I'd nurtured for so long, she took her time, her movements deliberate and respectful, making clear that she knew how significant each pass of the scissors was for me.

My long hair had hung thick and dark and dead straight. When Loretta was done it was still thick and dark, but to my surprise, it was curly. For so long my hair had been a kind of talisman of my identity, a mark of pride that, in its own way, made me feel more Indigenous—visible and connected to a tradition I loved. I'd worried about losing that when my hair fell away, but instead I found a new and unexpected marker of my history and heritage: my short, dark curly hair looked exactly like my grandmother's. It was Ojibwe hair through and through, even if a family of German tourists or a cruiser full of white police officers would never be able to recognize it as such.

I long for the day when Indigenous people are free and equal enough for their hair to just be hair, when all racialized people can live without everything about their bodies and behaviours being politicized. That still feels a long way off to me, but in the meantime I know that I can always choose to let my hair grow again or keep it short, even buzz it off (if Julie will let me). For as long as it has jailed and killed us, colonialism has sought to strip us of our Indigeneity by removing its traditional visual markers. I will not let that happen to me. Regardless of how it's styled, my hair is the hair of an Ojibwe man. It ties me to my family and culture, my history and identity. It ties me to Norma.

CHAPTER 9

Radio? Really?

As I neared the end of my fourth and final year at U of T, I had a pretty clear sense of the next steps I was going to take in life. My plan was to graduate, spend the summer working in the warehouse at Scepter/Ipex, and then head to Humber College in the fall to study film and television production. Students at Humber were granted free access to the school's equipment for use on their own projects, which was the big draw for me. My head was full of film theory. I was itching to put it to practical use and finally start making movies.

The fork in the road arrived, as they often seem to do, completely by chance. While investigating some options for summer work, Julie saw a posting at the U of T job centre for an internship at the CBC. Supported by the NAAF and aimed specifically at Indigenous candidates, the placement was as an associate producer in the national broadcaster's radio division. When Julie told me about it later that day, my first thought was that "associate producer" sounded like a pretty fancy job (for the record, it's not the least bit fancy). Sure, it was radio and not TV or film, but I wanted to be in media. Here was a chance to get valuable experience and make a few useful connections before heading to Humber.

The big hang-up for me was the same one I'd faced just before university: *Should I even apply?* That nagging feeling of not being quite the right type of Indigenous person was still kicking around in my head, and it again gave me pause. But the arguments my mom had made for the original NAAF scholarship application process still held up and held sway for me, so I ultimately went ahead with it. After I was chosen I found out I'd been one of just four applicants, which helped me shake the worry of having denied dozens, even hundreds, of other Indigenous youth an opportunity. I don't feel a lot of residual guilt over the whole thing, but as I write this I realize that I do still feel a need to explain myself, to minimize any perception of having hurt the community or taken something from another Indigenous person—especially someone who's suffered more or been offered less.

I know on an intellectual level that this whole muddy stew of identity and emotion is an intentional consequence of white supremacy. That there are so few opportunities available is a result of large-scale racial and economic inequality; it's the fault of the system, not of the precious few people who receive those opportunities. But it's a feature of white supremacy to always make people of colour feel guilty about any opportunity or advantage we get. We're also conditioned to take up that cause ourselves, to nitpick, shame, and judge one another. Rigging things so completely that even the meagre opportunities that exist are set up as tools of separation, potential wedges to drive between you and your community and you and yourself—that is a nifty trick. It's also a remarkably powerful one, seeing as I'm fully aware of it and yet still suffer from its effects.

There was little time for self-flagellation once the CBC job began. It was a four-month placement, with my time split between chasing stories for national syndication, which was known as Infotape, and contributing to a Toronto afternoon radio show called *Later the Same*

Day. It didn't take long for me to realize that an associate producer's job was largely composed of the grunt work no one with any seniority wanted to do, but it also challenged me in ways I found genuinely engaging.

Radio syndication involved arranging and producing interviews that could be picked up by local stations across the country. I'd find stories, track down guests, write the scripts, and then feed interviews to show after show—each guest running through the same conversation many times in a single day. We'd also cut tape and write scripts around that existing audio for shows to use.

The other half of the internship, working mostly behind the scenes on *Later the Same Day*, was an amazing learning experience in that it allowed me to see how to build a full show rather than the discrete segments I'd been creating in syndication. And the program itself was a dynamic one, hosted by a woman named Katherine O'Hara (not the more famous Catherine O'Hara). It had so many moving parts that it was fascinating to witness how they were all brought together in a cohesive whole. Katherine and the lead producers were adventurous, too, and gave me chances on the air that I'm not sure I would've gotten anywhere else. I remember covering the opening of a Planet Hollywood restaurant and deciding to be a real smartass by poking fun at the celebrities attending. When I got back to the office I was lightly scolded by one of the producers, but Katherine loved the segment. "The best part," she told me, "was when you made fun of Bruce Willis."

The need for content to help fill twenty-four hours of programming every single day opened up opportunities like that fairly regularly. During my time at Infotape I pitched a column based on the booming home-video market, and was given the go-ahead. Each week I'd review three old movies grouped into a theme: elections, say, or back-to-school. The segment was pre-taped and sent out for any station that wanted it. Surprisingly, people liked it, even though I was still figuring out how to talk on the air. Other opportunities arose thanks to the

CBC's stinginess. When the longtime film critic for *Metro Morning*, a wonderful man named Jack Batten, took a leave of absence to write a book about the founding of the Toronto Raptors, I happened to be the intern who'd recently graduated with a cinema studies degree. Some may have questioned the wisdom of handing over a regular role on Toronto's flagship morning show to a kid with just a few weeks' experience—none of which was in live radio—but no one did at the ever cost-conscious CBC, at least not loudly enough to stop it from happening. I was told to write a five-minute-long script and to show up to record it during the six a.m. hour. When the host, Andy Barrie, threw to me, I was to start reading my script and not stop until I was done. Those were the only real instructions.

I was terribly nervous before my first appearance—live radio, it turns out, is considerably more nerve-racking than anything pre-recorded. Andy delivered my introduction, ". . . and here's Jesse Wente," and then, as I launched into my reviews, he opened a newspaper and began reading, seemingly paying me no attention whatsoever. I was so new to radio that I thought this was normal—how the sausage is made—and just tried to focus on getting through my script without flubbing a line. It wasn't until I worked with other hosts that I realized the newspaper was something unique to Andy. When I finished and threw back to him, he folded it away and picked up as though he'd hung on my every word. Before I'd even had a chance to register it, I was a working film critic.

The CBC internship I'd landed had been created specifically to bring in aspiring young Indigenous producers, but that didn't mean any noticeable increase in the broadcaster's appetite for Indigenous stories. In the four months my placement lasted I worked on only a single project that specifically addressed the Indigenous community or Indigenous issues. That the story at its centre was absolutely unignorable may have gone some way toward explaining how it got the traction it did.

In November 1996 the Royal Commission on Aboriginal Peoples released its final report. A culmination of five years of work begun in the wake of the Oka Crisis, the report not only attempted to encapsulate the whole of the past and evolving relationship between Canada and First Nations, Métis, and Inuit people, but also proposed a twenty-year plan for addressing and resolving many of the issues faced by Indigenous people in this country. Given that scope, it's a miracle of efficiency that it clocked in at a mere four thousand pages.

As the date of the report's release approached I was still working on *Later the Same Day*, the only Indigenous person on the show's staff; despite my inexperience, I was asked to take the lead on producing our coverage and then left almost entirely alone to execute it. I suppose that decision could be seen as tokenism, and maybe it was. It didn't feel that way at the time, though.

Tokenism, to my mind, is representation without agency; it is a co-opting of Indigenous identity for the gain of non-Indigenous people without allowing those Indigenous representatives the ability to make decisions or effect change. I would go on to experience it plenty in my career—that feeling of being made a symbol of something without actually being that thing—but in this case I was actually given the power to produce the segments as I saw fit. I wasn't speaking on the air, so I wasn't being held up as a token—at least in a public sense. Was it ideal that I was an intern who'd just graduated film school and possessed no formal journalistic training? Clearly, it wasn't. It illustrated the shameful underrepresentation of First Nations, Métis, and Inuit among journalists and media members. But at least I was actually Indigenous, and at least I was actually doing the work.

That said, my being asked to helm the coverage was indicative of the way the Royal Commission was ultimately treated by Canadian media and the Canadian public: as something to be given passing acknowledgment and then ignored. This was a major commission whose work, they felt, could be adequately summarized by an intern, meaning that *I* may not have been a token but that the Commission itself was—something that's only been reinforced by the media's and governments' reception of subsequent efforts like the TRC and MMIWG. Such commissions and inquiries have done plenty of meaningful work, and it's disrespectful to those who participated in and shared their truth that these reports too often end up as trophies on the government's mantelpiece. When people's demands for action are inscribed in written documents, these documents get held up as evidence of Something Being Done— as symbols that stand in for meaningful change. That may not be openly acknowledged in the coverage the media accords them, but it's certainly clear in the care and attention put into their production.

Even if I didn't feel tokenized, the experience did make me realize that my Indigeneity could be something sought after, if even for just a moment, and that performing it was something people would want me to do. I suppose that knowledge could have made me feel valuable or in demand, but instead it was terrifying. I was still figuring myself out, working to better understand my own identity. Yet here, as I entered my professional life, it was obviously expected that I'd brought my community with me, that I was there as a representative.

To this day I remain reluctant to speak on behalf of the Indigenous community. It is a group too big, too varied, too rich in ideas and opinions for any one person to feel confident in having their finger on its pulse. I've always been willing to speak on my own behalf, but at that nascent stage of my career I didn't feel equipped to speak responsibly for *any* larger group (with the lone possible exception of movie nerds), let alone one I was just starting to discover my place within.

At the same time, I was always conscious of the fact that I might not have much choice in the matter; that even if I didn't make any grand claims myself, anything I said publicly could be framed as a representative opinion rather than an individual one. People of colour wear their communities in a way that white people don't. No one would ever assume that a white person's thoughts could stand in for their entire race, but people of colour are regularly asked to accomplish exactly that feat.

In addition to your thoughts, your failures are projected onto others as well. On some level, hiring a person of colour is still seen as a risky proposition—maybe just because it's unfamiliar. If an Indigenous person is brought in to do a job and they turn out to be bad at it, well, that might be taken to mean that no Indigenous people will ever be able to do it—*why risk making the same mistake again?* There has been a looming sense with everything I've done in my career that "I better do it well because I don't want to become a future barrier to entry for anyone in my community." I take that responsibility very seriously. I do not want to let my community down, either by speaking some bullshit supposedly on their behalf or by failing in my work. These are stresses I can't imagine many white people facing.

The extra weight people of colour are made to carry is the reason I've tried to make sure that my Indigeneity was never the point of my being on the radio, that I was paid to be a film critic on the air because I was a damn good film critic—full stop.

When the internship came to an end, I had my home-video column and what seemed like an increasingly steady spot on *Metro Morning*; plus, I was offered a three-month contract to stay on at the CBC. Still, I held onto the idea that I'd go to Humber and eventually start making movies. But those plans were derailed. First, Julie had decided to go back to school to study law and we figured it might be best for one of us to have an income. Second, and much less practically, it's a pretty cushy job to go see a movie and then be paid to voice your thoughts about it. It was fun, and I felt like I was a part of the film industry—even if it wasn't in the capacity I'd imagined when I was in school.

Jack Batten finished his book and came back for a while, but the producers eventually moved on when the show went through a refresh. I was officially hired as the film critic at that point, initially alternating weeks with Cameron and Maxine Bailey before that dynamic brother-and-sister duo took on senior leadership roles at the Toronto International Film Festival. Behind the scenes, after nearly two years of living three-month contract to three-month contract across a variety of departments, I was hired full time as a producer for *The Arts Report*, a daily arts-focused newscast hosted by the veteran broadcaster and respected dance critic Michael Crabb. I later moved on to produce *The Arts Today*, a national arts show hosted by Eleanor Wachtel, who was also host of the hugely popular literary program *Writers & Company*.

It was a fun and busy time. Not only was I producing long-form interviews with some of the world's most prominent artists for a host who was a tremendous interviewer; I was also enjoying a regular spot on the top morning show in Canada—along with an excuse to watch all the movies I could handle. I felt, if not fully established, then well on my way. I felt happy and comfortable and capable. And I felt that I was finally in a place where I had something real to give back, where I could make good on the promise I'd made my mom before I went to university. It was time to turn back to my community.

CHAPTER 10

Finding My Footing on Native Earth

My mom has always been averse to having her picture taken. Among the few that exist is my parents' wedding photo, and in it, the first thing you notice is my mother's hair—long, black, and hanging down her back past her waist. (My dad's hair, it's only fair to note, is also at its peak, shoulder length and curly.) In the photo they're young and instantly identifiable as the hippies they were—or rather, in my mother's case, the proto-hippie: a First Nations woman, an identity to which much of hippiedom aspired, or at least co-opted through its fashions and hairstyles.

I don't remember my mother with that long, beautiful black hair, hair that so unequivocally told the world who she was. She cut it short around the time my sister came along, a practical choice dictated by the realities of being a working mother chasing after two young kids. It was also—though I suspect not as intentionally—a choice dictated by her professional aspirations. She would eventually climb from her starting position as a clerk at Con Chem Ltd. to a senior executive, having to smash at least two glass ceilings on the way. It's safe to say that nothing came easy and no one handed her anything. Under those unforgiving circumstances, cutting off the hair that had marked her so undeniably as an Ojibwe woman may not have helped, but it certainly couldn't have hurt.

When I cut my own hair decades later it was for different reasons, but at some level the result was the same: our ability to be white-coded, or at least white-coded-enough, allowed us to sidestep some of the issues faced by those Indigenous people who more closely match the mythical Indian of popular culture. Short hair made existence a little easier.

This is far from the only way my path has mirrored hers. Like me, my mom was largely distanced from the Indigenous community for much of her younger life. Yes, she visited the rez regularly, but she had no Indigenous friends she wasn't related to and she wasn't active, at that point, in the fight for First Nations, Métis, and Inuit equality. As was typical for much of her generation—the children of residential school survivors, some of whom were survivors themselves—the trauma her mother endured had a direct and significant effect on her own sense of identity. But as I think is also typical of her generation, she eventually experienced a political and cultural awakening, reconnecting with the community she'd lost and becoming quite radical in her thinking later in life.

This awakening seemed to kick into gear after she started volunteering with Indigenous organizations. Practising what she'd preached to me as I debated my application for the NAAF scholarship, when she reached a certain level of accomplishment in her career she turned back to the community. She sat on the board of the Native Canadian Centre of Toronto, of Nishnawbe Homes, and of many other organizations dedicated to improving the quality of Indigenous life and helping the least fortunate. Her executive experience was a deeply valuable asset; she did, and continues to do, a tremendous amount of good. And through her involvement with these organizations and causes she began to make more Indigenous friends and was brought more fully into the community.

When I set out to fulfill the obligation to give back to my community as my mother had urged, it didn't occur to me that I'd get so much in return. It's easy when you're first volunteering for a charity or an arts organization to feel a bit saintly, framing the situation in your mind as you giving of yourself while expecting nothing in return. I was soon disabused of that notion, though, because when I turned back to my community, I found it waiting with open arms and the most beautiful gift I've ever received: a better sense of who I am, and an understanding of what I was put on this planet to do.

My mom didn't just inspire my volunteer work; she was the link that landed me my first opportunity in that area. A friend of hers, Frances Sanderson, sat on the board of Native Earth Performing Arts, the oldest professional Indigenous theatre company in Canada. Whether at my mom's direct urging or simply because she felt that any kid of Connie's wouldn't be a complete nincompoop, Frances, a lifelong activist and organizer who founded Nishnawbe Homes, invited me to join the board.

This was in 1999, less than a year after the CBC brought me on full time. I was young to be on the board of an arts organization and the first to admit I knew nothing about theatre, but there had been some measure of accomplishment in my career. I'd gained a public profile through my regular appearances on *Metro Morning* (and later *Q*) as a film critic and pop culture commentator, and as a producer on *The Arts Today* I was relatively embedded in the Canadian arts world. Another point in my favour—possibly outweighing anything on my CV—was the lack of Indigenous professionals available to sit on boards.

I was already involved with the Toronto Police Chief's Youth Advisory Committee, but Native Earth instantly felt different. On the police committee I was the only Indigenous person and as such expected to speak for my community, yet the work gave me no real avenue for figuring out how to do that or even what to say. As I talked about earlier, it was uncomfortable. I was being asked to act as a spokesperson when I sometimes felt as if I were barely a member of the community at all. So I mostly stayed silent—a shock to anyone who knows me today, I'm sure—and the experience became little more than a minor but consistent source of guilt.

Native Earth, on the other hand, may have been small and in turmoil when I arrived, but it was an Indigenous company. Yes, I was still asked to be a representative for my community—representing the Indigenous experience was and is one of the mandates of the company, after all—but for the first time in my life I was surrounded on a regular basis by Indigenous people I wasn't related to. That proximity alone was reassuring and invigorating. I was able to form real, personal connections with Indigenous artists and others in that world, which made me feel like less of an interloper. And when that feeling of not belonging, of being the wrong kind of Indian, did crop up, I now had a network of fellow Indigenous people to help me set my head back straight on my shoulders.

Those relationships were important to me, because, early on, I wasn't all that sure what I had to offer. I mean, take my sister Maggie, who's incredibly smart and an academic achiever: having earned her law degree, she now works to defend and uphold treaty rights, spending her days battling the government in court in the name of Indigenous rights. She's a total badass, and I couldn't be prouder of her and the work she does. And yet my own path to that kind of positive impact wasn't so clear. I'd accepted the role on the board at Native Earth because it was offered and I was eager to help, but at that point I often wondered to myself, "I love movies and I'm a geek. How do I turn that into something that's empowering for the community?" It was through my exposure to Indigenous art and artists that I started to find an answer.

My introduction to the company, just prior to Frances's offer, had itself been revelatory. I'd been invited to a performance of a play called *Annie Mae's Movement*. Written by Yvette Nolan, who'd go on to become Native Earth's artistic director, it told the story of Annie Mae Aquash, a Mi'kmaq activist who was part of the American Indian Movement and whose murder in 1975 remains unsolved, variously attributed to the FBI and to AIM itself. Just as *Incident at Restigouche* had forever changed what I thought movies were and could accomplish, Nolan's play completely altered my understanding of theatre. Through her work I saw that our lives could be dramatized, that we could be the story, and that it could be a damn good story.

Native Earth was home to giants like Nolan and Tomson Highway. Here were unbelievably talented people telling stories of Indigenous life and experience—stories I'd never seen anywhere else but that I soon understood were as entertaining as anything Hollywood could produce and so much more powerful because they shared a truth rarely seen. I ended up serving for many years as the president of the board.

It still took time for me to fully realize the role I had to play, but in the end it wasn't a particularly complicated one. How can a movie geek help to lift up their community? By supporting Indigenous storytelling in all possible ways. So by the early 2000s I was doing everything in my power at the CBC to not only shine a light on Indigenous filmmakers in my on-air work but also to seed the shows I produced and the news-rooms I worked in with Indigenous voices.

Ultimately, though, I wanted to do more. In my on-air work I'd always aspired to criticism rather than just reviews; instead of stopping at a straightforward consumer service I wanted to engage with the art itself, aiming to push it forward by provoking reflection and meaningful dis-course. That wasn't always possible, of course—some movies are just so bad you can't do much more than warn people to stay away—but I felt I'd mostly managed to remain true to that goal. The problem with criti-cism, though, is that it's easy for people to ignore, especially when you're advocating for something they've been conditioned their whole lives to ignore: namely, the voices of Indigenous people. That problem was only exacerbated by the rise of the internet. Don't get me wrong: I'm all for dismantling traditional systems of distribution (even if they've been good to me) and giving a voice to those so long shut out of the mainstream media. But when everyone on the internet became a movie critic, it significantly diluted the impact of criticism. Now you could be ignored and drowned out simultaneously.

Critics are placed in a passive position in relation to the art they critique, judging finished work, watching the movies the industry has already deemed important enough to make and promote. But what about the stories that weren't getting made, the artists who existed outside the machinery of the industry itself? What about the movies that were shot on a shoestring budget through pure ingenuity and then struggled to find an audience?

In 2005 I was invited to join the board of imagineNative, then embarking on its fourth annual film and media arts festival. At that time one of the board's committees programmed the festival, and I was asked to help specifically with that effort. Here was another fantastic opportunity to throw myself behind Indigenous storytellers. Programming also seemed like a way to have more direct influence over what was prioritized and supported in the film industry—that is, which films executives, distributors, audiences, and indeed the critical community itself got to see. Sure, I'd still be dealing mostly with finished films, but the choices of what to champion would be so much wider and deeper. Instead of relying on what happened to be opening in theatres that week, I could be part of the process that determines which movies open in the first place. I would go on to program at the Reel World Film Festival as well.

It's impossible to overstate how much this board work gave me, how much it shaped me as an Indigenous person. In my first few years at Native Earth I met and befriended many creators, thinkers, and activists. That network of support and inspiration only grew through my work at Reel World and, particularly, imagineNative, which allowed me to see the global nature of the movement for Indigenous rights and culture in a new way and exposed me to amazing filmmakers from around the world, people whose work it was virtually impossible to see anywhere else in Canada.

These new friends and mentors made me feel like a full-fledged member of the community for maybe the first time in my life. They also profoundly influenced my thinking about history, politics, and the issues facing Indigenous peoples, both directly and through a kind of osmosis of ideas. As far back as I can remember I'd felt a tension between my sense of self and the way I saw Indians portrayed in movies and on the news. In high school I'd tried to find the words to express that feeling. But the people I met through my board work actually talked to me about that tension, having known it in their own lives; when they inspired me to read the works of activists and intellectuals like Art Manuel, John Trudell, and Lee Maracle I discovered a rich vein of Indigenous writing I'd left untapped. And when they inspired me to read the laws and acts that had established the framework of the relationship (at least the legal one) between Indigenous people and Canada, I discovered the lies this country is built on. They gave me the words. And eventually, they gave me the courage to speak them publicly.

For years my work as a representative of the Indigenous community had been almost entirely behind the scenes. It wasn't something that played much of a role in my radio columns, and at Native Earth I understood that I was there because I brought other things. As I moved more fully into programming roles, though, I was increasingly asked to speak publicly on behalf of the organizations I was working with. It's common practice at film festivals for the organizers to offer some explanation for the movies they're presenting—to champion the work and provide the audience with necessary context. The person programming the lineup tends to be the one who stands up and offers these explanations, and I was the one doing the programming. Just by pure function, then, I ended up on stage speaking on behalf of Indigenous organizations.

That was still not a comfortable situation for me. I mentioned before that from time to time I still struggle with feelings of inadequacy, of not fully belonging. I was worse back then. What saved me and saw me through was the acceptance of the artists. Again and again I was encouraged to step out and speak on their behalf. I may have felt like an interloper, but they made it clear they didn't share my opinion; they showed me one of the great generosities of the Indigenous community: our deep understanding of why people end up where I did. They knew it wasn't my fault I'd grown up distanced from the community, even if I myself felt that way from time to time. They didn't hold that distance against me; they understood my confused and conflicted experience and they loved me—in spite of it and because of it. They welcomed me with open arms.

The more public-facing responsibility I was asked to take on, the more my voice grew. And as I learned more about the community, I developed a better understanding of how to speak for it—the processes through which to best ascertain the message people wanted delivered. I became more assured that I could speak without saying the wrong thing, without doing damage.

It helped, of course, that I was deeply passionate about the work I was asked to speak for. By the mid-2000s I was convinced that the tension and lies in Canadian culture that so maddened me could best be addressed through First Nations, Métis, and Inuit art—that having Indigenous stories more present and more heard would counterbalance the only story allowed to exist on a national or even global scale. And it may not sound like it, but a fair amount of faith in Canada was baked into that idea: a hope that this country could somehow become welcoming. Although there wasn't a lot on my mother's side of the family to inspire that belief, my dad did manage to instill some of it in me. He would say that having come to Canada from the U.S. was one of the great strokes of luck in his life. The pain and injustice he's been exposed to because of who he married aside, I think he saw Canada as a more polite, more caring place. So there's a part of me that even now thinks, "Boy, wouldn't it be great if Canada could be what it presents itself as?"

Despite that glimmer of hope, I've never had a real sense that change could come from Canada itself. My thoughts weren't necessarily well-formed, but some part of me has always known that only Indigenous voices speaking with the power I first witnessed in *Incident at Restigouche* could bring true understanding to this country. That gave me a strong place to speak from as well as the energy to continue on despite a truly ludicrous workload, which included upholding my responsibilities at the CBC, throwing myself into my volunteer work, and watching as many as fifteen hundred movies a year. I could do it because I believed in the power of Indigenous storytelling—and because some movies were so obviously and immediately bad, especially the ones from Hollywood, that I didn't have to watch them all the way through.

In 2006 I was offered a position on the Toronto International Film Festival's Canadian features programming team, largely on the strength of my work at imagineNative and Reel World (though I'm sure my growing radio profile didn't hurt either). It was an incredible opportunity, a spot at one of the most prestigious film festivals on earth. So, even though it meant leaving my full-time job at the CBC, I jumped at the chance, made all the sweeter by being assured of having a real voice at the table. I'd made a mark as a critic (and would continue doing weekly reviews), but it was my advocacy on behalf of Indigenous filmmakers that seemed to have really won over TIFF's leadership. Ensconced in an institution from which it was possible to make a real impact on the industry, I'd be in the best position I'd ever had to advocate for Indigenous storytellers.

What could possibly go wrong?

CHAPTER 11

This Ride Costs One Token

Over the course of my career I've been in a lot of spaces where I was the only Indigenous person. That was the case on *Later the Same Day* when I covered the Royal Commission's report, it was the case on the Police Chief's Youth Advisory Committee, it was the case in newsrooms and on production teams throughout most of my time behind the scenes at the CBC, and it was also usually the case in my on-air work—if you'd spun the dial in the mid to late nineties, how many Indigenous people would you have found on the radio in Toronto? Few, if any, besides me. Throughout my decade-plus in criticism, I was the only working Indigenous film critic in Canada (and possibly in North America, though I never made an exhaustive survey). Culturally and racially, I was almost always an island of one in my work—often the only Indigenous person to ever occupy the role.

Though it didn't feel like a blessing to be alone in that way, I *am* deeply thankful for the opportunities I've had. They've allowed me to do a lot of work I was and am deeply passionate about, and have granted me insights into the actual nature of Canada that other Indigenous people may not ever get simply because they're barred from those same positions and spaces. Of course, the counterbalance has always been the knowledge that I must truly be the Acceptable Indian to be allowed entry in the first place.

Knowing I'm the exact type of Indian that residential schools were designed to produce and that I'm considered tolerable by a system bent on eradicating Indigenous existence is an uncomfortable, even painful, thing to live with. It's not an identity I aspire to; it's been imposed, and imposed in a way meant to seduce, numb, and coerce me into playing along, into fully embodying the image of an Indigenous person in which I've been cast. I've had to deal with that imposition a lot in my life, and my first step in managing it has always been to ask myself a simple question: Are you going to actually be the Acceptable One, or are you going to raise hell and find a way to weaponize your privilege against the very place that's given it to you?

I've opted for weaponization wherever possible, and if that seems an unnecessarily aggressive or combative choice, I'd like to point out that in addition to the slurs, fists, policies, laws, media narratives, and actual weapons brought to bear with regularity on Indigenous people, privilege itself is weaponized against us from the moment we receive it. As I felt in the case of the NAAF scholarship and internship, it's used as a wedge to further separate us and our communities, to instill guilt and resentment. And it's always given with the expectation of payback in the form of assimilation, of happily holding up the system that oppresses us. Truly, colonial powers give us nothing that they don't take back in at least equal measure.

Indigenous lawyers, like my sister, provide a great model for weaponizing privilege because that's exactly what they do every day of the week. *Train me to the best of your ability so that I can show up in your courtrooms and win using your own laws.* I think some version of dismantling the system from the inside is what so many of us in the movement for Indigenous rights are doing. We can't help where we landed in the history of this country and of our communities. That generational trauma may have driven us from our cultures, languages, and families is not our fault. That our disconnection may have been accompanied by access to opportunities that would've been inaccessible on-rez or by another Indigenous person isn't our fault either. Our privilege doesn't mean we should feel too ashamed to participate in our communities, to give back to them; nor does it mean we owe anything to the colonial powers that provided it. We were born into the circumstances we were born into, we jumped through the hoops, and rather than making us forget who we are and the people and cultures we come from, it's made us only more determined to remember and connect. If the system did everything in its power to pull us in and win us over and we still want it destroyed, that's the system's failure, not ours.

When I was hired by TIFF, I was again in the position of being a first and only. In this case I was the first Indigenous programmer the festival had ever had. It was a demanding workplace, intensely political and competitive, and I carried the extra weight people of colour are all too familiar with: I was a stand-in for my entire race, meaning if I messed up it might make me the last Indigenous programmer as well as the first. I was up for those challenges, even invigorated by them early on, but I also knew that I could succeed beyond anyone's expectations and there might still never be another Indigenous person afforded the opportunity. So before I'd even set foot in the building I determined that, while I had any say in the films shown, I was going to make damn sure the Canadian section featured more Indigenous films and filmmakers than ever before.

Things got off to an auspicious start on that score. In my first year with TIFF, the festival opened with *The Journals of Knud Rasmussen*, the second film in the Northern Trilogy of Zacharias Kunuk, the director and producer best known for *Atanarjuat: The Fast Runner*. *The Journals* was the first, and remains the only, Indigenous film to open the festival. While I certainly can't claim credit for that decision, I was in the room when it was made and was given the time and space to explain why I thought the choice was both a deeply important one and the *right* one.

Two years later, I would program the third film in the Northern Trilogy. Produced by Kunuk and written and directed by Arnait Video Productions, an all-female Inuit filmmaking collective, *Before Tomorrow* casts first contact with Europeans as an intimate apocalyptic horror story. It screened at Scotiabank Theatre in downtown Toronto, and I remember being profoundly moved to hear Inuktitut in a big commercial multiplex. I think I cried when it started playing.

I was also determined to be a critical voice where the festival's larger programming was concerned, and to do everything I could to stop them from screening films that I thought were hurtful or damaging to the Indigenous community. I'd been promised a real say, and as I started out I found that to be the case. I wasn't just taking up space; I had a voice in the room. I was there to be heard, and my opinion was respected. It felt like I had the power to do real good. It would be a long time before that changed.

I'd been a contract festival programmer at TIFF for about four years when I got a call one day from Noah Cowan's assistant asking me to lunch on his behalf. Noah, the person who'd hired me for the Canadian features section, had recently taken on a new role as artistic director of the festival's so-new-it-was-still-under-construction year-round venue at the corner of King and John, just a block north of the CBC broadcast centre in the heart of Toronto's theatre district. Apart from being present one day when they brought in a bunch of cinema chairs for us to test out and vote for our favourites, I hadn't been privy to many details about the new space, one that would eventually be called TIFF Bell Lightbox.

I'd first encountered Noah more than a decade before I joined TIFF, back when he launched the festival's Midnight Madness program. A showcase for genre cinema, it was exactly the type of thing a horror-obsessed movie geek like myself would love, and was the program that attracted me to the festival in the first place. Always interested in challenging the canon and accepted wisdom and taste, Noah had been very supportive of me as a programmer, especially when my choices were a bit outside the norm. An excitable, bombastic, whip-smart force of nature, he was someone I'd always liked.

I had no idea why he wanted to get together this time, but I knew that at the very least I'd get a good conversation with the meal. Over lunch at a salad-centric restaurant, we talked about our families and the movies we'd recently seen before a slight shift in Noah's tone and posture signalled that I hadn't been invited for pleasantries alone. It was time to get down to business.

Noah asked me how much I knew about the new building, the Lightbox, and whether I knew anything about their plans for the space. When I admitted that I didn't, he laid out a vision for an unrivalled art house facility, with five public theatres, two gallery spaces, and a new home for the Cinematheque Library, a place where I'd spent a lot of time as a film critic. He said there'd be two restaurants, concessions, educational spaces for students, and a gift shop on the ground floor. All of it would be centred on movies. And during the festival proper, the major event of the year, the Lightbox would be TIFF's beating heart.

He basically described my heaven. A temple to movies.

He told me he needed to hire someone to help run the building and oversee the film programming, and asked if it felt like something I'd be interested in.

I paused before responding, not because I needed time to consider my answer but because, frankly, I could hardly believe this was happening. Was Noah presenting me with what seemed like my dream job?

He was. And he was waiting for an answer.

I told him it sounded amazing and that I would definitely apply.

In the days after that lunch, I sent off my résumé along with a pair of writing samples. One of the pieces I included was a recent review of

King Kong, as directed by Peter Jackson. It wasn't the type of film that would ever get shown at TIFF, but I was particularly proud of that review, with its references to cinema history and contemporary Hollywood. And it must've done the trick, since I was called in for an interview.

Noah was there, of course, along with Cameron Bailey, the festival's co-head, whom I'd first met when we were both critics, and Piers Handling, the CEO who'd been in charge for more than a decade. They asked about my thoughts around programming, what I could imagine seeing at the venue, and my vision for what a modern art house movie theatre could be like. And then they asked what career retrospective I would most want to put on at the Lightbox.

I answered George A. Romero, of course—the zombie-movie king who'd inspired Tal Zimerman and me all those years ago. I explained that I thought Romero was the father of an entire genre—one that was only growing, as we were still several years from the debut of *The Walking Dead*—and that his defining characteristic, beyond giving ample screen time to the undead, was that his films were political and very purposefully so. Romero embraced the idea of horror movies as a way to explore significant cultural issues, from racism to consumerism to totalitarianism. I told them I thought his films, contextualized as political works, still had vital relevance and would draw a crowd to a theatre. Plus, he had plenty of personal and professional connections to Toronto.

Now, Romero was not the type of filmmaker who had typically headlined the Cinematheque that TIFF operated year-round. James Quandt, the founder of Cinematheque and a hero of mine, preferred the masters of Asia and Europe; through his programming I'd been introduced to Yasujirō Ozu, Kenji Fukasaku, Henri-Georges Clouzot, Michael Powell and Emeric Pressburger, and many others. I had no idea whether my answer was the right one—or, at least, the one they were looking for—but it was an honest one. For me, there'd always been good movies, bad movies, and a few great movies, and entries in each of those categories came in all shapes, sizes, and genres.

That was really the vision I presented: a temple to cinema should be a temple to *all* of cinema—the good, the great, and occasionally, when the time is right, the bad. I imagined a place where Ozu and Romero could live side by side with the latest in cutting-edge movies from around the world. What I was pitching was my dream movie theatre and, in fact, the sort of screening schedule I tended to run at home, where classics lived alongside all manner of cinematic weirdness.

I left thinking it had gone well and simultaneously thinking I had no idea how it had gone. I had no experience running a movie theatre and had never programmed for a Cinematheque; surely they would be interviewing people who'd done exactly those things. I tried to resign myself to the fact that I probably wouldn't get it.

It was only a few days later that Noah called. "How'd you like to come work with me at Lightbox?" he asked. I could hardly believe it.

"I'd love to," I told him.

It's no fun being a token.

I know, I've been one more than once. I may be one right now.

If that "may" throws you, if it seems as though the difference between being valued for your work and being valued as a symbol would be obvious, then let me tell you: it can be surprisingly hard to tell when you're being tokenized—at least in the short term. After all, you do still have an apparent value. People seem to want you around. You're made to feel involved in things. You also may be genuinely qualified and bursting with good ideas. It can take time to realize that those qualifications don't matter to your bosses and coworkers, and that nobody intends to act on anything you say—that you're there for show.

You may have become a token only over time. You may have been listened to at first. Your ideas and ideals may have been respected and appreciated right up until the point when they required someone to take a stand or a personal risk, or until they required cost, sacrifice, or accountability. It can take even longer to realize that you aren't being listened to if you were listened to at some other, earlier juncture.

Canada has a tokenization problem, one sadly and inextricably linked to the image of its national character that it presents to the world. This country has always wanted to be seen as a kind, gentle, loving place, as a peacemaker and peacekeeper, and it has tapped Indigenous communities and Indigenous cultures to help sell this point on the international stage. At the 2010 Vancouver Olympics, for example, Indigenous cultures were front and centre. Our art, music, dancing, and traditions were all on display. The reasons? First, because they *are* beautiful; they deserve to be showcased to the world because they're world class, much the way individual Indigenous people who end up being tokenized are often well qualified. But the other reason for pushing us forward was to sell a lie: that we are embraced by Canada the Good; that this is a nation that celebrates and honours its First Peoples.

The wrench in the works of this narrative machine is the truth of Canada's relationship with Indigenous communities, its colonial past and present. We're publicly celebrated while behind the scenes militarized police storm our sovereign territory to force through land developments and oil pipelines; while we're again and again denied economic and educational opportunities; while our communities go without clean drinking water. As Thomas King wrote in his classic book *The Inconvenient Indian*, this country and its colonial powers aren't interested in actual Indians, just the idea of them they've conjured. They want our land, our culture, our hair, our skin, our sovereignty, just not us. They want us to make them look virtuous in the eyes of the world at the same time as they work to erase us.

It's common to find Canadian politicians adorned in the finery of many nations while at the same time voting against Indigenous interests again and again. There is perhaps no better example of this hypocrisy than Prime Minister Justin Trudeau himself, who before he was elected to the highest office in the land was known to wear buckskin and hang around canoes, and who famously sports a tattoo on his shoulder that's based on a Haida design. Trudeau was first elected in part on the promise of a renewed relationship with First Nations, Métis, and Inuit, one grounded in nation-to-nation relations. It was a compelling pitch to a population that genuinely wants to see glaringly obvious inequities resolved. Yet Trudeau has largely governed the relationship as other Liberal governments have done, namely by allowing Indigenous people to suffer in order to aid the advancement of the settler state.

In one of the least ironic displays in Canadian political history, Trudeau even beat up a First Nations person as a way to advance his career. In 2012, then serving as the member of Parliament for Papineau, Quebec, Trudeau beat Patrick Brazeau, a Conservative senator from Kitigan Zibi, in a five-round charity boxing match that was broadcast on live television. The drubbing propelled Trudeau, a legacy politician following in the footsteps of his father (who introduced the deeply racist White Paper in 1969, seeking to end the treaty relationship between First Nations and the state), to the leadership of the Liberal party and, ultimately, the PMO.

We are tokens to be cashed in on the way to Parliament Hill.

So it should be no surprise that, in the Age of Reconciliation initially embraced by Trudeau, Canadian institutions have approached us in the same shallow way. In recent years they've come to understand that having some Indigenous representation is important for their public image. We now see Indigenous people being hired at universities, in government, in the arts and media. These hirings and appointments are, in many cases, the result of decades of advocacy and activism around inclusion and representation. They're the result of people who worked twice as hard to get half as far and who somehow made that awful math result in something tangible and uplifting. People who fought for their positions, fought to retain them, and in doing so helped create the space for others to follow. I've benefited from this history, and I hope I've continued that work.

But the gruelling fight that rewards you with an uncomfortable place as the only Indigenous person in the room doesn't do anything to diminish the threat of tokenization—or the reality that it may be the only reason you were allowed through the door to begin with. In the post–Truth and Reconciliation Commission era, Indigenous representation has become the one path many organizations can see to that reconciliation. Yet although there's been lots of talk and indeed hiring around the idea of decolonization or Indigenization, many of those hired have left before completing their terms. We're to be trotted out when needed but then put away as soon as we actually speak out or, God forbid, ask for actual change to occur.

Tokenization is a byproduct of dehumanization. It's hard to tokenize someone you see as fully human, someone whose ideas and work you respect. As such, its ubiquity is a measure of how societies, cultures, and nations view specific groups. It's not easy to walk away from something you've worked your whole life to achieve, but it's close to impossible to stay once you realize that your worth ends at mere representation.

In my experience, no matter how well disguised the tokenization, that realization always comes eventually, and it's never once been fun when it arrives. At TIFF it took years, and it ultimately ruined the job of my dreams.

I started full time at the beginning of 2010. With ten months to go before the new building opened, it was still little more than a concrete shell, requiring significant imagination to visualize in its final form. Despite the lack of clarity around the space itself, though, my main priority was clear: figure out how to run a movie theatre.

That crash course would turn out to be an exhilarating, if hectic, ride. In my first months on the job I was sent to Cannes and New York to learn what I could, first at the world's premier film festival and then at the IFC Center, a hugely successful indie cinema. In France I drank rosé, took meetings, and watched movies in equally exhausting numbers, meanwhile trying my best to make myself comfortable in a vastly expensive and claustrophobically tiny hotel room. And when that famous festival was in full swing, I also experienced a surreal metaphor for the film industry as a whole: the red-carpet glamour of the Palais du Cinéma backgrounded by an ocean view dotted with multimillion-dollar yachts contrasted against the Marché, a global marketplace for movies in what was formerly a pornographer's bazaar beneath the Palais.

In New York, after visiting Film Forum, the Museum of Modern Art, Lincoln Center, and the Angelika—a whirlwind tour of film geek highlights through the city's legendary art house scene—I and a couple of colleagues connected with John Vanco, the industry veteran who runs the IFC Center. Extremely generous with his time and ideas, John showed us the ropes, from how the centre ran front of house to how they approached marketing. It was eye-opening and utterly inspiring. John scheduled the films, the staff, everything, from a single spreadsheet on his computer. These were Jedi-level Excel skills the likes of which I'd never seen. He also explained his philosophy of exhibition, the kinds of movies they showed, why they scheduled the way they did—all the tricks of his trade.

I arrived back in Toronto thinking I knew everything. All it took to prove me wrong was the actual opening of the building. We were instantly underwater—overscheduled and understaffed. Those first six months were some of the busiest and hardest of my professional career.

Over time, though, as TIFF built the capacity to properly run its theatre, we found our feet. By the end of 2011, Lightbox was the number-one-grossing indie cinema in Canada and one of the top-grossing independent cinemas in all of North America. We'd figured it out. I was running a theatre, watching movies every day, and working with some of my artistic heroes.

Connecting with filmmakers and engaging with movies never got old. So as the demands of the job—and of the festival's political infighting, which was so intense that navigating it often felt like a job unto itself—wore on me to an increasing degree, it was the joy of those exchanges about art and artists that I clung to in order to convince myself that I was still happy at TIFF, that it was still my dream job. In truth, I was miserable much of the time. But looking back, it scares me to think how long I might have ignored that dejection if that same old ugly realization hadn't hit and made the situation truly untenable: the powers that be had lost the will or interest to engage with my ideas and had come to see me as a token to be deployed at their convenience.

First, I was asked to help write a land acknowledgment for the festival. I'd been doing one at my events since the opening of Lightbox. It was 2017, and they'd become more common throughout Canada since the Truth and Reconciliation Commission's final report a little more than a year and a half earlier, but TIFF proper didn't yet have one codified.

Land acknowledgments are exactly what they sound like: a recognition that you're visiting someone else's land. It's very much how Indigenous people tend to introduce themselves: name, Nation, maybe family. It's a way to contextualize yourself so that everyone can understand where you're coming from. For non-Indigenous people it serves as an effective reminder of the history of the place they occupy, their relation to it, and the obligations that should come with sharing this land. A land acknowledgment is a statement of relationship, and it should be underpinned by an actual relationship in order to have any real meaning. Unfortunately, in practice they've now largely become performative and perfunctory—a token nod to a relationship that doesn't actually exist.

Taking the request as an indication that the organization was ready to embrace the Indigenous community in a new and meaningful way, I adapted the acknowledgment I'd been using and turned it in, hopeful that it would inspire a moment of reflection in those who heard it, eager to see what the festival's larger efforts to connect with Indigenous life might look like, and excited for something that couldn't be stripped of meaning as easily as I'd seen land acknowledgments could be. As

I waited for even a hint of those efforts to materialize, I had plenty to keep me busy.

The work of screening films to be included in the next year's festival began almost as soon as the previous year's festival wrapped. As you might imagine, determining what was worthy of selection involved watching hundreds of movies. And you'd think that in that crush of cinema only the absolute best would stick in the mind. In 2017, though, three films that were far from favourites would lodge themselves in my head. They were *Hostiles*, *Woman Walks Ahead*, and *Indian Horse*.

All three films are about Indigenous people and yet made by non-Indigenous people. Rather than seeking them out or stumbling across them, I was specifically asked to watch each one. Private screenings were arranged specifically for me to see them. I watched two of the three alone.

These screenings came in the midst of a national discourse on cultural appropriation in which I'd featured heavily—something I'll address later in the book. I'd been speaking very publicly about the issue and, in doing so, I'd begun to feel somewhat exposed and unsafe, even in my professional capacity at TIFF. At the same time I was running a monthly screening series called *Aazbingawashi*—which means "wide awake" or "cannot sleep" in Anishinaabemowin—that had received the bare minimum of support from the festival.

Wrung dry by the painful public conversation and feeling unsupported in the meaningful work of the screening series, it was an emotional and difficult time for me. And here I was, after all of that, being asked by the organization I'd worked with for more than a decade to make sure I watched movies about Indigenous people that weren't made by Indigenous people—a pretty obvious example of appropriation and a pretty clear indication of their priorities. The writing was creeping up the edge of the baseboards; after seeing the films, it would be right there on the wall.

Although unified by their cultural theft, the three films differed from one another in a few key ways. *Indian Horse* was Canadian, while the other two were American movies with big stars. In addition, *Hostiles* was what's known as a "sales title," meaning it was still seeking distribution. These titles often get priority at the festival because TIFF can count them as part of their industry impact if they're sold to a distributor. Even though TIFF consciously decided not to have an official marketplace like the one in Cannes, during the time I was there it nonetheless courted the opportunity to be seen as a place where movie business gets done. In the name of that priority, sales titles would often get the best slots so that they'd be more visible to buyers.

Woman Walks Ahead stars Jessica Chastain as Catherine Weldon, a portrait painter who in 1890 travels to paint the portrait of legendary Lakota leader Sitting Bull, played by Michael Greyeyes. The film is fine but astonishingly bland, leaving the viewer with little more than a rather rote biopic that's soft on truth and even softer on history. Weldon is centred, rather awkwardly, against the backdrop of Sitting Bull's much larger struggle. At one point she's labelled an "Indian-loving bitch" by a racist Indian agent, an offence framed as more significant than the ongoing oppression of the Lakota. It's a classic white saviour movie. In my note to the rest of the programming team I said it was soft in all ways and fell on familiar tropes that, to me, served no one particularly well. I wasn't overly offended by it, but I *was* exhausted by it.

Hostiles, on the other hand, *that* I was offended by. A western in the classic mould, starring Christian Bale in what had been positioned as an Oscar-worthy role, the movie follows a Confederate veteran—one who brags of his exploits at Wounded Knee, where the U.S. army slaughtered more than three hundred Sioux—after he reluctantly agrees to escort an old enemy, a Cheyenne chief played by Wes Studi, back home.

Along the way, Bale's army captain falls in love with a woman and is forced to defend the people he's spent years trying to kill. It's a redemption story of a Confederate soldier and murderer of women and children that grants its Cheyenne characters little, if any, dialogue, despite having actors as accomplished as Studi and Adam Beach among the cast. At the end—

COLONIAL SPOILER ALERT—all the Cheyenne are dead and the army captain and his love ride off into the sunset in the back of a train, a literal representation of Manifest Destiny.

My note for the film was harsh. I said flat out that it shouldn't be shown, that it was deeply racist, both in its story and its construction, and that it engaged in the worst kind of myth-making. I noted that the Indigenous characters had no agency, little humanity, and little purpose beyond advancing the story of the white characters. And I argued that it was exactly the sort of movie that should no longer be made; that it did nothing more than reinforce a myth that has done remarkable harm to Indigenous people.

I felt I'd been pretty clear.

Indian Horse, the last of the three, was an adaptation of a truly fabulous book by Richard Wagamese about a boy named Saul Indian Horse, who, after the death of his grandmother, is forced into residential school, where he endures sexual abuse that haunts him for years. It's a deeply emotional and beautifully crafted book, and one that spoke to me directly, as Saul could have been any of my uncles and great uncles. I'd long felt it deserved to be brought to the screen, but had been disappointed when I heard it was being adapted by a non-Indigenous director. Although the movie was nicely shot and acted, the direction felt at a distance from the source, the grief of the story displayed rather than felt by the film. To me, this was what made it obviously not an Indigenous film. For all its craft, it felt disconnected from its subject. It was a tragedy beautifully rendered, but not lived.

Wagamese's untimely passing before the movie was completed meant he wasn't around to discuss its limitations, nor to confirm how involved he'd been. In my initial note on the film I described it as okay but not great. I said I wished we weren't still making these sorts of stories this way in Canada, but added that at least it wasn't actively racist, like *Hostiles*. I never advocated for it to be kept out of the festival; I just pointed out that it represented a production model we needed to move away from.

The final decisions around what to include lay with the program-ming teams and, ultimately, Cameron Bailey. At the end of the summer I was told that both *Woman Walks Ahead* and *Hostiles* had been selected.

When I heard, I said they should just show *Indian Horse*, too. "Why punish a well-intentioned but flawed Canadian film if you're going to let outright racist work from America into the festival?" I asked.

As they searched their hearts for an answer—and a decision on *Indian Horse*—a senior executive from Elevation, the company distributing the Wagamese adaptation, called to tell me they'd been given the impression that I was the reason the film hadn't yet been selected. I wasn't officially part of the Canadian programming team, nor the festival team at all, and yet I was still being used as a fall guy for their decisions. Worse, there was a good chance they'd put my name forward to avoid any possible accusa-tions of anti-Indigenous bias.

I'd been asked specifically to weigh in on these "Indigenous" films only to see my strongest recommendations completely disregarded. I'd seen my name and identity co-opted without my permission in order to make a decision I had nothing to do with harder to criticize. And while special screenings had been scheduled for me to see movies like *Hostiles*, no efforts at all were being made to ensure that I saw actual Indigenous work. If I wanted to see those movies, I had to seek them out myself. This despite the fact that TIFF was happy to note the presence of the world's foremost expert on Indigenous cinema on their staff. In short, I was being asked to watch appropriative films while the work I wanted to engage with was kept at arm's length and remained the purview of non-Indigenous programmers.

It had taken eleven years, but just like that I was a token. Whatever agency I may have once had was gone. I'd been made to watch these films that were not my responsibility, asked to weigh in on their value and ultimately their ethics, and when I did, my feedback was ignored. Those films would play, and in the case of *Hostiles*, the most egregious of the three, in the prized seven p.m. slot on the opening Saturday of the festival—perhaps the most valuable slot in the entire schedule. Worse, it would play after a land acknowledgment that I had crafted and advocated for. I felt it was a deep betrayal; they were going to acknowledge Indigenous lands and then show movies that minimized Indigenous people or that existed without their equal participation.

Since my thoughts on these movies would never be public, and since I wasn't able to comment publicly on my colleagues' programming decisions, it could appear to my community that I had approved of these films. They were being shown under my watch. TIFF would be able to say that its foremost expert on Indigenous cinema had screened each film, but I wouldn't be able to say what I really thought about them. And that was it: I knew my time at the festival was over. My position there wouldn't hold any meaning for me or for my community if it was nothing more than a token. In that capacity I would end up doing more harm than good, providing cover for an organization's poor choices while allowing them to feel and appear inclusive and progressive.

I submitted my letter of resignation shortly before the festival began.

PART III

The Stories We Tell Each Other

CHAPTER 12

Learning to Live with
Death Threats

I got my first death threat in 2016, the year before I left TIFF.

It was waiting for me on the answering machine at home. A private number. A male voice. "Shut up or get scalped," he said. "You don't know what the fuck you're talking about." And then a click as he hung up.

I listened to it twice, standing beside the cluttered corner computer desk in our basement. As the message played for the second time, my gaze drifted to the surface of the old Arborite kitchen table that served as a printer stand, wedged in next to the desk. My body went numb as I stared at the first piece of furniture Julie and I had bought together, those awful words striking out at me through the earpiece.

"Shut up or get scalped."

That morning I had delivered an emotional radio column about the harm caused by Indigenous sports mascots. I was responding to a piece in the *Toronto Star* newspaper that labelled such concerns and the efforts to address them—such as banning clothes bearing the mascots' likenesses in Toronto schools—as political correctness run amok. It wasn't a new or surprising argument; this kind of entitled demand that we prove the damage done to our communities, the crimes committed against us, is as familiar as the denials and deaf ears our explanations are ultimately met with. It was an argument born from a place of wilfully blind privilege, a position so ignorant and fraudulent that it was hardly worth engaging. But it was also an argument that did real harm, one that had the potential to incite more hurtful and harmful action. So, despite the apparent fruitlessness, I engaged.

The form this engagement took was sadly familiar, too: an enumeration of simple, irrefutable facts, widely available to anyone, that certain white people nevertheless seem unaware of and unwilling or unable to hear. I pointed out that Indigenous mascots were racist, and had always been racist; that far from being the tribute their defenders occasionally framed them as, an argument deployed in the *Star* piece, they were damaging symbols of oppression first used during a time when North American colonial powers were engaged in active genocide of Indigenous peoples. I pointed out that we are not mascots, we're human beings. Immediately after the segment aired I got support from many listeners, especially teachers, who said they'd use the column in their classes, and that kind of positive feedback always makes me happy. But that wasn't what was on the answering machine.

"You don't know what the fuck you're talking about."

That the information I'd imparted—I won't call it an opinion, because it was all fact—had inspired someone to find my family's unlisted number and threaten my life was, of course, a surprise, and a deeply unpleasant one. But it was the intensity that caught me off guard more than the reaction itself. Radio is an intimate medium. People listen when they're waking up, when they're stuck in traffic or doing the dishes, when they're in the shower, when they're getting the kids out the door in the morning. It's that intimacy that makes it so effective for storytelling, why you can use it to reach people in a way that nothing else really can. And that power can also spark passionate responses—both positive and extremely negative.

I realized this power and potential fairly early in my career, and out of respect for it I'd always been cautious about how much I revealed on the air. The pieces of myself that I did share were carefully chosen, meant to enrich my reviews with flashes of humour, depth, and humanity without ever centring my identity. After all, I was there to talk about movies and pop culture, not myself.

Occasionally the *Metro Morning* crew would stage the show as a live performance—usually around the holidays to raise money for local charities. During one Christmas broadcast Andy Barrie brought out each of the columnists to say a hello and deliver a few quick lines. At one point he asked me what my favourite Christmas movie was. "*Die Hard*," I responded. "You say 'Merry Christmas,' Andy; I say 'Yippee-ki-yay . . .'" I didn't finish the line, as that would have put a quick end to my radio career, even if it would have been a legendary moment. The crowd laughed knowingly.

That was my sort of thing, leaning into my geekiness. It let listeners know who I was without actually telling them anything personal. I'd mention my kids but never name them; I'd talk about Julie but never in a way that revealed anything. That I was Indigenous also came up here and there, but not as a central feature in any of my work. I was known as the movie geek and the video-game guy, and I liked it that way. Wanting my life off-air to be *my* life, I kept the facts of who I was vague and piecemeal. I worked that way for the first thirteen years of my career before a single review changed my approach and, ultimately, turned me into a different kind of columnist and public figure. Because after seeing James Cameron's *Avatar*, there was no way I could hold my tongue.

By the time *Avatar* arrived in the winter of 2009 I'd been a film critic and pop culture columnist for more than a decade. I was working freelance, appearing on more than twenty-two radio shows a week for the

CBC (all recorded in a marathon session each Friday), programming for TIFF, and volunteering as the president of Native Earth Performing Arts. Over the years I'd become deeply engaged with the Indigenous community in Toronto, largely through my work in the arts, and despite being someone who'd never imagined a career on the radio, I like to think I'd become a pretty good broadcaster, too.

I'd reached a place in my career where I felt confident in my abilities and secure in my position—both at CBC and TIFF. My new job running the Lightbox would start in a few months, plunging me back over my head into a whole new learning process, but for the moment I was comfortable; I knew what I was doing. I was busy, to be sure, but I'd also climbed high enough to take a few easy breaths and survey the landscape.

I was still a relatively new parent, too, and those two beautiful little Ojibwe babies had awakened in me a new level of community responsibility. No longer was I living or working or loving just for myself, and that knowledge pushed me toward a more activist way of looking at the world. It shouldn't take having children to spark a real desire to make the world a better place, but for me that was key.

In retrospect, then, it feels like I saw *Avatar* at the perfect moment— that, in many ways, I'd spent my entire movie-watching life waiting for it. What's funny is that I felt the same way at the time, too, only for completely different reasons. Here was a blockbuster that looked to be as close to *Star Wars*, my beloved childhood obsession, as any movie made since. Directed by a filmmaker I quite enjoyed, one with many excellent, state-of-the-art science fiction films already on his résumé, *Avatar* had been anticipated for years before it arrived, heralded as the film that would usher in a new age of moviemaking centred on immersive sound and high-resolution 3-D. I expected to engage with it as a movie nerd and sci-fi fan, and I did, but ultimately I would read—and despise—the film as, first and foremost, an Indigenous person.

The screening was held in a massive multiplex theatre in Toronto's downtown core, just a block north of the still-under-construction

Lightbox. The turnout was substantial, and as the city's critics shuffled in, there was a buzz in the air befitting a major moment in film history. We found our seats and slipped on our 3-D glasses. The lights dimmed.

I've always loved the feeling of sitting in a dark theatre surrounded by people—the hum of anticipation as the opening credits roll, the communal laughs and tears, shock, recognition, and pathos. That sense of shared experience is part of what drew me to the University and the Fox, the cramped, smelly screening rooms in the Eaton Centre's revolutionary multiplex, the eye-opening Cinematheque, and so many other theatres over the years. And when I first began as a film critic it was hard to imagine that my work would take me to places capable of uniting total strangers and bringing them on a shared journey. It felt like, and was, such a privilege.

It didn't take Cameron's film long to sap that sense of interconnectedness right out of me. Within the first twenty minutes I was convinced I was watching a different movie from damn near everyone else in the room. In the flickering light from the screen, I saw rapt faces. I overheard murmurs of awe and approval, my colleagues marvelling at the film's slick technological achievements and the novelty of its approach to 3-D. The feeling in the theatre was one of undisguised enjoyment. Meanwhile, I was radiating anger.

The film's central action revolves around the effort to relocate an Indigenous population, the Na'vi, whose existence on the faraway planet of Pandora is standing in the way of a massive resource extraction project aimed at securing a vital fuel called "unobtanium"—yes, that's the actual name. In case that setup doesn't get the point across, these blue aliens, who stand ten feet tall and have tails, are festooned with the clichéd trappings of the Hollywood Indian—feathers braided into their hair, revealingly scant animal-hide clothing, bows and arrows, headbands. When going into battle they war-whoop like a children's softball team. They're referred to as "native," "indigenous," and "aboriginal" throughout the movie—another not-so-subtle hint at the film's allegorical intent—and they physically connect to their natural sur-roundings through their long braided hair, making any environmental destruction a threat both socially and individually.

Though the multi-galactic mining conglomerate heading the extrac-tion project is the film's antagonist—see, it's not *all* bad, there's an intended indictment of environmental violence, war, and colonialism—the Na'vis' only chance of defending themselves and their way of life comes in the form of a white man who uses advanced technology to remotely operate a lab-grown Na'vi body. He is literally wearing Indigeneity as a costume. This revolting form of "going native" climaxes in the inevitable way, with the white saviour out-Na'viing the Na'vi. He taps into their ancient spirituality in a way none of the Na'vi themselves seemingly can, and uses the planet's natural energy to save the day, "chosen one" style.

The plot is a mess, based on some of the worst tropes of the Golden Age westerns, and that outmoded narrative made *Avatar* feel oddly dated even ahead of its release, when it was undoubtedly a state-of-the-art technological event. The film itself, as I would later say in my review, is an expensively rendered colonial fairy tale. It reduces the Indigenous peoples of the Americas to a prop that showcases white excellence and capability. It reduces our identity to a garment that a white person can wear so convincingly that it fools even us. It reduces millennia of spiri-tual practice down to something a "well-intentioned" white person can comprehend better than we ever could in just a matter of days. As I predicted in my review, *Avatar* would go on to become the highest-grossing movie of all time. And as I also noted, it was an enormous step back for Indigenous representation in film.

About three months before *Avatar*'s release, *Reel Injun*, a documen-tary about the history of Indigenous representation in Hollywood, premiered at TIFF. Its director, the Cree filmmaker Neil Diamond, had interviewed many experts in Indigenous cinema, including me. Our conversation, seven hours stretched over two days, was both comprehensive and cathartic. Beginning with the very earliest images captured by Thomas Edison—of Sioux performers—we moved through the Red Westerns made by the East German state and right up to the rise of Indigenous cinema globally, along with everything else we could think to touch on in between. Hollywood's depiction of Indigenous people had always leapt out at me in painful ways, and I'd devoted much effort to trying to understand the effects movies have had and continue to have on Indigenous people. After all, they shape how we're perceived—or not—by mainstream culture.

Reel Injun offered a clear and damning condemnation of Hollywood's failures. When it earned critical praise and commercial success, a part of me felt that its existence would stop people from making movies like the ones we criticized. That, somehow, one small Canadian documentary would fundamentally change Hollywood. Hey, remember, I've always believed in the power of movies.

Sitting there seething through the *Avatar* screening, I took a moment to quietly kick myself for ever believing that Hollywood could do better. When I walked out of the theatre after the final credits, I was too upset to talk. There's an unspoken rule among critics that you don't share your opinion coming out of a film for fear of swaying your colleagues or of their swaying you. As we made our way across the lobby and down toward the exits, then, there weren't any in-depth discussions of what we'd just seen, although I did hear the odd "Oh, wow" and saw the amazement in my fellow critics' faces. I knew right then that the review I'd write wasn't going to be at all like theirs. They hadn't seen the movie in the way I'd seen the movie—not even close—and honestly, that wasn't particularly surprising.

Since I'd started working as a reviewer, I'd been the only Indigenous critic in Toronto. As far as I could tell I was the only one in the country— at least with a regular, paying gig. One of *Reel Injun*'s distinguishing characteristics is that, other than the directors Clint Eastwood and Jim Jarmusch, all the on-screen experts are Indigenous. Most of them are filmmakers or professors; I was the lone working film critic featured in the documentary. To this day I've never met another Indigenous critic, a fact that has always made me despair.

The presence of at least one other Indigenous critic wouldn't have guaranteed that someone else in the room read *Avatar* the way I did, of course. But the absence basically guaranteed that no one else would. White supremacy, cemented into the foundation of Hollywood just as firmly as any other major North American institution, does not equip white people to recognize the faults that leapt out at me as I watched the film. When racism doesn't harm you personally, noticing it requires conscious effort, or at least empathy—just as acknowledging that you benefit from racism requires you to acknowledge its existence. White supremacy deters and clouds this effort in so many ways, reinforcing white people's place at the centre of things in all facets of life and discouraging any thought of those who are pushed to the margins. It is a propaganda campaign waged against all of us from pretty much the moment of our birth, and it encourages white people to look away by tangibly rewarding them for doing so—often in ways they aren't even aware of. Film criticism, as is common in professions of privilege, is overwhelmingly white. So, with a lack of diverse voices and white critics conditioned their entire lives to be blind to messages like the ones embedded in *Avatar*, it's really no surprise that my opinion of the film differed so obviously and immediately from my colleagues'.

To be clear, I don't blame white critics, at least not individually, for seeing a glitzy technological marvel and little else. It's a bit disappointing that they didn't recognize what the film was actually saying—if more of them did, movies like this might not get made—but it also would've been shocking if any of them had.

I also don't think Cameron himself realized he was making a racist film, or consciously intended to incorporate racist elements. I think he thought he was being respectful, that he was making an environmentalist allegory and an anti-war movie. But like many filmmakers before and after him, he managed to make something racist almost by accident because he didn't consider Indigenous people as whole people. He may not have had racist intentions, but he certainly didn't have anti-racist ones—he didn't examine himself and his project for biases; he didn't seek to hire and empower people with a better understanding of these issues; he wasn't open to uncovering and addressing his own ignorance—and in a white supremacist system like Hollywood, anything that's not intentionally anti-racist has a chance of turning out racist.

The same is true in almost every institution and field of endeavour in North American life: if you're not striving toward anti-racism, there's a good chance you're participating in a racist system, indirectly or directly. I have a lot of patience for white people who struggle with that idea, because I understand that almost nothing in their lives equips them to recognize or cope with the truth in it, and I know it can be deeply uncomfortable to have your worldview upended. If you think of yourself as a good person, someone who's never done anything racist, I can see how difficult it would be to come to grips with the fact that you can allow, facilitate, and even participate in racism without ever realizing it—and that you likely have done those things.

I can also imagine how having that pointed out would feel like an assault on your sense of self. I learned how painful that type of attack can be as a ten-year-old on the Topham Park baseball diamond, and I've felt it again and again throughout my life—from store owners, police, friends, total strangers, and, of course, movies and TV shows. So I have sympathy for the resulting pain and confusion, even if their cause is justified, which wasn't the case in the attacks on me. And because I have some sense of these feelings, I'm not all that surprised by the typical response.

Every time I've pointed out racism and white privilege in my career I've tried to move from the specific inciting incidents to larger systemic problems. Rather than sticking the blame for racist actions on individuals (though they're far from blameless), I've worked to show

how those actions result from and reinforce larger systems of oppression. Yet again and again the response I've seen from many white people is to assign themselves individually into the systems being critiqued, to centre themselves and their experiences, to perceive and react to something personal instead of the larger social commentary. In this framework, criticizing a racist mascot is seen as calling every individual fan of that team a racist; pointing out that BIPOC are disproportionately harmed by police is seen as calling all officers racists and murderers; asserting the value of Indigenous lives is seen as attempting to devalue all other lives; and acknowledging white privilege is seen as claiming that no white person has ever experienced hardship. This tendency is one of white supremacy's great defence mechanisms. It recentres white experience in conversations about the lives of racialized people, and it creates a personal stake for each individual white person in maintaining racist systems and structures—not that they don't already have those. If people can hear criticism of the mascot of a team they don't own or play for as an accusation that they're racist, then how open can they be to a call for the mascot to change?

In addition to white people's tendency to think of everything through the lens of white experience, I think this feeling of being individually attacked or held to account comes from the underlying knowledge that they benefit from a system that harms others. If they didn't feel the truth of that somewhere, there'd be no way to be offended by it; if they didn't know the extent of their privilege, they couldn't recognize the gravity of the crime. Individualizing the offence is a way of trying to deny that knowledge, of putting space between themselves and the racist systems from which they benefit—and the more desperate that effort, the more vehement their offence and the more certain they are, deep down, of their own culpability.

These mental gymnastics are also often accompanied by attempts to turn away from the issues completely and to force others to do the same. As an argument or attack, this manifests in far-too-common refrains. BIPOC who point out racist hiring practices, for example, are accused of perpetually playing the victim, of "making everything about race," of trying to get a job based solely on their skin colour—as though white people haven't been doing just that for hundreds of years; as though BIPOC aren't regularly denied jobs for the same reason. Indigenous people who for decades called on teams like the Cleveland Indians, Atlanta Braves, Chicago Blackhawks, Edmonton Eskimos, Kansas City Chiefs, and, of course, Washington Redskins to change their racist names were consistently told to "keep politics out of sports," even when the murder of George Floyd finally set those changes in motion. How could we possibly do that when those very names show just how deeply the dehumanization of Indigenous people is embedded in all levels of sport? How could one not think sports leagues had made themselves political long ago by excluding people because of their race? To celebrate the integration of baseball as a political moment while claiming that any criticism of the racist representation that persists within the game amounts to politicizing the sport is the exact sort of hypocrisy that white supremacy encourages and emboldens.

In settler-colonial states, where white supremacy is at the core, it's only white people who can depoliticize at will, who can decide not to be affected by things and have that wish come true. Whether I speak openly on the issue or remain silent, Indigenous mascots harm me; if a Black person chooses not to point out the micro-aggressions he or she faces every workday, it doesn't magically resolve the situation. What these calls to avoid politicizing everything really ask for, then, is for BIPOC and women and LGBTQ2SIA+ and any other marginalized group to suffer in silence, to avoid even asking those with privilege to think of its human cost. And the fact that the anger of the privileged when we don't keep quiet, when we simply ask them to acknowledge the truth, can burn so hot that they find our unlisted numbers, call our homes, threaten our lives—that, to me, shows how fragile their grip is, how toxic their fight to keep hold.

"Shut up or get scalped. You don't know what the fuck you're talking about."

When the message finished playing through the second time, I deleted it—as I would later delete the other threats. I didn't want Julie to hear it and worry, which was true but also the reason I repeated in my head to drown out the other reasons. "Protecting her" was more palatable to me than admitting that I simply didn't want the message to exist, anymore or ever, and that erasing it would at least mean I never had to hear it again. And it was far more palatable than facing down the fact that I felt guilty I'd received the call and didn't want anyone to know it had happened. Much like my interactions with the police in university, I felt as if I were to blame, even though I was the victim. I felt as if I had invited violence into our home.

White people, you can depoliticize and retreat to a place where the rest of us can't go, and there's a certain kind of power in that fact. But I think the greater power lies in confronting your privilege and the ways you benefit from the subjugation of others, and working to correct the systems that gave you so much at the expense of so many. I know that's a scary idea, to be open instead of running away. I know it will force you to come face to face with an image of who you are that could cause you great pain and confusion. And I know that some of you would rather threaten violence, or even commit acts of violence, than look in the mirror. And I know that deep down you know that I know what I'm talking about.

Usually I'd review three movies in my five-minute segment. The logic was that reviewing two big studio pictures would allow me to highlight something I thought was important for the audience to pay attention to with the third slot, which was usually how I seeded Indigenous content in my columns. For the *Avatar* review, I let my producer know that all five minutes would be spent on the one movie. When I filed my script the night before we went to air the response I got was, "Wow, this is . . . going to be interesting."

As I've noted, the fact that I was Indigenous had probably come up before in my columns and appearances, but it had never been a central feature in a discussion. So I knew that this review could potentially change my professional identity forever; that after fighting so long to be taken on my merits as a critic rather than pigeonholed as "the Native critic" I might, in five minutes, be pigeonholing myself. But I also knew that *Avatar* would be a pop culture phenomenon, and that most people who saw it would miss its racism unless they had it pointed out to them. I was more anxious about going on air than I'd been in years, and yet I felt that the substance of the review had to be my reaction to the film as an Indigenous person. If I didn't include more of myself than I was truly comfortable revealing, the point wouldn't land with the same force.

So I said what I said. I began by praising Cameron's technical prowess and correctly predicting that *Avatar* would be the biggest box-office success of all time, and then I gave voice to my anger and pain and described the immense harm the film would do to Indigenous people. Any remaining anxiety evaporated as I spoke, and in the end I thought the whole thing had come off very well.

Back then, my routine was to go for breakfast at a diner near the CBC building each week after my *Metro Morning* appearance. That week I'd barely made it out of the studio when messages started rolling in from First Nations people who'd heard the piece. By the time I was out on the street I knew the reaction to this column was different from any other I'd ever delivered. Indigenous people from across the country, including people I'd idolized in the arts, were reaching out to tell me how happy I'd made them. Again and again I read some version of "I can't believe I heard that, thank you so much. It's unbelievable that you just did that."

I'd always been extremely reluctant to speak in a way that could be taken as "on behalf" of the Indigenous community. The sense of having no right to claim that voice linked back to the feeling of not being

Indigenous enough or not being "the right kind" of Indigenous person—a feeling I've known most of my life and still can't fully shake—but it also came from a recognition of the folly of any one person thinking they could speak for a group so vast and varied. But as I sat there in the diner, waiting for my breakfast, I was able for the first time in my life to think, "If people are going to be okay with me going on air and talking this way, then I feel safe doing it."

As the messages and emails continued to roll in, I saw just how many in the First Nations community had yearned to hear that kind of response to a major Hollywood event, and how many felt I'd been their champion. I didn't need to hear from any other community after that; I'd heard the only opinions that mattered.

Heading into the studio, I'd feared how that review might alter my career. Looking back, though, I can see how it acted as a turning point, one that, instead of pigeonholing me, opened up new worlds to explore. It showed me how I could speak for myself while also bringing my community along. How I could use my platform to speak against the injustices Indigenous people face in this country and around the world, and how that effort would be met with solidarity and gratitude. I am so thankful for that support and trust. I am so thankful for each of the messages I received that day, and for every message a First Nations person has sent me since. They give me the courage and energy to continue this work. They guide me in the right direction. They let me know that I'm not alone; that everything we face, we face together. They show me that no threat, no hate-filled person, can shut us up. They remind me that we speak the truth.

And when that truth is finally acknowledged, meaningful change can spark and spread like fire.

After years of protest, advocacy, boycotts, and endless arguments on social media, it seemed that overnight the mascots began to disappear. In July 2020, after a short "review process" and under pressure from sponsors and shareholders, the Redskins became the Washington Football Team. The Cleveland Indians followed with a commitment to re-evaluate the team's nickname—widely seen as a first step toward doing away with it. And later in the month, the board of Edmonton's CFL franchise announced that it would no longer be using the Eskimos name.

All it took to finally achieve this change was the single largest racial equity movement since the heyday of the 1960s fight for civil rights. All it cost were the lives of far too many Black and Indigenous people at the hands and weapons of the police. I have no idea how history will judge that sick accounting, but should anyone in the future claim it was worth the price, I'm writing here to say it was not.

Racist team names, logos, and mascots are the low-hanging fruit of social justice—the easiest things to change. Names and logos change all the time. I've lived through more iterations of the Coke and Pepsi brands than I can remember. And although there may have been criticism highlighting the stupidity of changing the flavour at some point, I don't remember anyone getting death threats over the particulars of the "Pepsi Globe."

Of course, those brands don't uphold the most necessary part of capitalism in North America: white supremacy. So perhaps it's no wonder the daggers don't come out when those logos and others like them are altered. No, the symbols worth fighting for, worth threatening violence for, in a society built on white supremacy are the ones that assert dominance and dehumanize, that allow some to feel superior even as they watch a kid's game.

Nations like Canada and the United States understand the power of symbols as part of the identity building and myth-making necessary to distinguish themselves from their colonial parents and disguise their own illegitimacy. By simply existing, Indigenous people challenge settlers' right to be in these "new" nations. Our presence is a constant reminder of the crimes committed to seize and hold these lands, crimes that are, of course, ongoing. Thankfully, our existence is ongoing as well, but Indigenous mascots work against that fact by attempting to replace us with a representation. They erase our communities by relegating them to the past, making us so much a part of the past that they've named their teams, cars, and military units after us in a bid to "honour" us in defeat. As well as vanishing us in the present, these symbols rewrite history in the colonizer's self-image, wiping the collective memory of the atrocities committed against us. The fact that these names and images have endured so long and been protected so vigorously isn't *despite* but precisely *because of* the racist ideas they represent.

With protests in the streets of most major cities over racial violence, though, that protection fell apart. In the face of such resounding calls for justice, changing these mascots and team names seemed an obvious capitulation. That fact shouldn't take away from the extraordinary solidarity that the Black community showed to Indigenous peoples. In a moment of such extreme trauma, with their family members being hunted by police, they made sure, while pressuring corporations for the removal of brands like Aunt Jemima and Uncle Ben, to fight for us as well.

Of course, moral outrage and calls for justice alone weren't enough to force these teams to act. The strategy employed was more savvy than pointing out right from wrong—and instructive in displaying both how capitalism benefits from racism and how undermining profits can bring change. By approaching sponsors and retailers like Nike and Walmart and hitting teams in the pocketbook, activists used the risk of financial loss as a way to force ownership's hand. More evidence of the strength of economic appeals came when WNBA and NBA players staged strikes within their respective COVID-19 bubbles, walking out for a couple of games and thereby spurring further action for social justice from their leagues and their teams' wealthy owners.

Still, it's not as though the same approach hadn't underpinned earlier efforts. First Nations communities had been advocating with sponsors for decades, and even long-standing attempts to stop the media from using offensive names and logos were rooted in the notion of devaluing them so as to reduce the teams' profitability. But Indigenous people are such a small proportion of the population in both Canada and the U.S. that boycotts extending only as far as our own communities seldom have national impact. It was solidarity with other communities of colour, specifically the Black community, that exponentially increased the impact and spread of these messages.

Of course, current social justice movements have large-scale aims far beyond the disappearance of racist mascots and brands, so to have any hope of achieving them, these same kinds of solidarity and economic strategizing will be essential. This is why the Defund the Police movement, as created by Black Lives Matter in the first half of 2020, is so clever and was so effective in changing the conversation. It appeals to people to consider the monetary cost of police and apply a cost-benefit analysis. Police are both extraordinarily expensive and, as I noted earlier, largely ineffective in what is positioned as their core mission: preventing crime. When the cost is considered alongside other elements of municipal, provincial, state, or national government budgets, the push to reallocate some percentage of police funding becomes an astonishingly persuasive argument.

Making an economic argument against the police, framing government budgets as moral documents, presents a choice to people who may not be affected by police violence but *are* affected by police budgets. This has helped the movement gain significant traction, shifting it from a fringe position to a topic of mainstream discussion in a matter of months.

The removal of racist mascots and brands had been openly discussed for a long time before it started becoming a reality. Financial considerations may have been what ultimately moved the needle, succeeding where moral arguments couldn't, but that doesn't change the fact that, along with efforts to eliminate monuments to slavers and Indian killers, these changes are a movement toward humanity and away from dehumanization. While moral appeals to those who have oppressed us have proven ineffective, that doesn't mean asserting our humanity isn't important, especially when it's affirmed in solidarity with other communities.

These are also multigenerational fights. The removal of these symbols is less about the relief of oppression today than it is about setting the conditions for the elimination of oppression in the future. My grandchildren will grow up in a world without these symbols; their absence then is more meaningful than their removal now. I'm so happy that they're disappearing in my lifetime, but even happier that, outside of historical displays and textbooks, my children and their children will never know them.

This is how we bend the arc of history toward justice—through heat and pressure like a piece of steel. This is the goal.

CHAPTER 13

The Power to Tell Our Stories

Richard Van Camp. Joshua Whitehead. Alicia Elliott. Tanya Roach. Louise Bernice Halfe. Elaine Wagner. Gord Grisenthwaite. Shannon Webb-Campbell. Helen Knott. Gloria Mehlmann. Kateri Akiwenzie-Damm.

I hope you will seek out these artists. They are the writers and editors featured in an issue of *Write* magazine, the official publication of the Writers' Union of Canada, that was published in the first week of May 2017. Each has had a profound impact on my life and on the larger cultural conversation in Canada, though that fact is often lost in the maelstrom that followed the issue. I've come to know some of them in the time since, at least at a distance, and my respect and admiration for them remains unbound. I would understand completely if you put this book down right now and went to find one of theirs—I guarantee it would be a good read.

The issue they appeared in was focused on Indigenous artists, a theme many cultural outlets and institutions highlighted in the lead-up to Canada's sesquicentennial later that year. It should have been a celebration of the remarkable literary work produced on Turtle Island by a diverse group of writers, both established and emerging. Instead, when these artists received their copies of the publication, they found their contributions accompanied by an editorial from then *Write* editor Hal Niedzviecki. In his piece, which opened an issue that, again, was theoretically meant to celebrate Indigenous writing, Niedzviecki not only suggested that cultural appropriation was a good thing, but also that perhaps there should be a prize for it. He even gave it a name: the Appropriation Prize.

I first became aware of the editorial when I saw the writers voicing their displeasure on social media. I took an immediate interest because by that point I'd been speaking for a few years about cultural appropriation and the damage it's done to Indigenous communities. I've talked about it plenty in the years since, too, and in my time engaging with this topic I've found that the human capacity to dissect just what cultural appropriation *is* seems limitless, especially when people start getting into specific examples: "Is a Pocahontas Halloween costume cultural appropriation?" "Is yoga?" The actual concept, though, is a simple one: cultural appropriation is exploiting a culture you don't belong to, and doing so without crediting, compensating, or properly consulting with that culture.

As is so often the case with the transgression that finally pushes people over the edge, the argument at the heart of Niedzviecki's editorial wasn't even an original one. He traded on the idea of freedom of expression, arguing that everyone "should be encouraged to imagine other peoples, other cultures, other identities," particularly writers. That may sound innocuous enough at first, but cultural appropriation's true nature showed through more clearly a paragraph later when he argued that the reason for the Canadian publishing industry's crushing whiteness was that the majority of published writers in this country are white, middle class, and afraid to write anything other than what they know. The solution to this, Niedzviecki contended, was for those same white, middle-class writers to write about other people instead of themselves. He went so far as to say that "[t]here's not even anything preventing us from incorporating a culture's myths, legends, oral histories, and sacred practices into our own work." Of course. Why create space for BIPOC to tell their own stories—stories so rarely heard—when white people could just take those stories and repackage them without credit for a white audience? Why show any respect for the sacred when its theft could make you a dollar? Again, this argument came in an issue of the magazine *focused on Indigenous writing*.

It was a tone-deaf piece of writing, and after being heavily criticized for it on social media Niedzviecki apologized and resigned his position at *Write*, stepping aside on Thursday, May 11. That's probably where the story would have ended if not for the fact that later the same day several of Canada's most prominent editors and print media figures took to Twitter to bemoan "the mobbing of Hal Niedzviecki," as then editor of *The Walrus* Jonathan Kay put it, and to mockingly begin raising funds for an actual cultural appropriation prize. Ken Whyte, former editor of the *National Post* and *Maclean's* and former president of Rogers's publishing division, kicked off the initiative, which garnered support over the course of the night from an imposing who's who of Canadian print journalism that included *Maclean's* editor Alison Uncles, *National Post* editor-in-chief Anne Marie Owens, Steve Maich, the man who'd succeeded Whyte as head of Rogers Publishing, and—one that had an extra sting for me—Steve Ladurantaye, then managing editor of CBC's *The National*.

What had started as a celebration of Indigenous talent in a creative industries trade publication had turned into an arrogant and uninformed pile-on about the nature and ethics of cultural appropriation. When I saw the tweets early the next morning, I responded with one of my own: "Just so we're clear, there already is an Appropriation Prize . . . it's called Canada."

Soon after I sent that tweet I was contacted by a producer with CBC's TV news department, who asked if I would appear on the broadcaster's cable news network the following morning, Saturday, to "discuss the issue" with Jonathan Kay. I hesitated to even consider the possibility. Kay had made his take on the situation abundantly clear the night before, describing Niedzviecki's resignation as "what we get when we let Identity-politics [sic] zealots run riot." What I was being asked to participate in wasn't a discussion, it was a "debate" in the unconstructive style beloved by TV news shows, one that often stems from a twisted notion of journalistic fairness being applied even to the sides of an issue that lack any real merit. Such segments also tend to favour known pundits to the exclusion of diverse voices, so you end up with media panels about race where all the panellists are white, for example, or about trans issues where no trans people are actually included.

I also didn't think it was a subject that could be debated—I still don't. I reject the premise that there are two sides at all. Cultural appropriation, as I'll get into in a bit, was literally written into law in Canada, targeting and decimating Indigenous communities in an official capacity for the better part of a century. To argue that it isn't a thing, that it's a false construct designed to limit free speech, is to be either wilfully ignorant or purposefully deceitful about the history of this country. Neither of those approaches is worth engaging with, in my opinion, so my first instinct was to turn down the request and, if I was so inclined, write about the issue for my next radio column.

However, there was an important issue to consider before delivering my answer. The involvement of Ladurantaye, a senior CBC producer, in the Twitter exchange meant that many of my CBC colleagues had been exposed to a reality about someone who had control over content at the network's flagship news program. That bias coming to light raised the very real possibility of the workplace feeling less welcoming and more uncomfortable for what was still a relatively small group of Indigenous employees. When I checked the page of a Facebook group for current and former Indigenous staffers at the CBC, I saw that the issue was already front and centre, and that that particular discomfort had been raised numerous times. Many had expressed the need for something to be said to the CBC about a member of its own senior staff involving himself. I wrote that I'd been invited onto the CBC News Network to discuss the issue and asked whether people on the page wanted me to accept. They said yes, making it clear that they didn't care about any "debate" with Kay or address to the public—they wanted me to use the CBC airwaves to send a message to the CBC itself.

In many ways, I was the most logical choice. I'd been a freelancer with the CBC since I left my staff position in 2006. That made it easier to criticize the place than it would for a full-time employee who'd have to fear retribution—it can be career-limiting to speak out publicly against the place where you work. My column was also popular enough to offer the type of security typically reserved for only the most senior columnists, a group that was, and remains, predominantly white. Finally, as a columnist, I was paid to give my opinion, something journalists are expected to refrain from doing in a profession based on reportable facts. Simply put, I was protected in ways most of them were not, and with that in mind, I agreed to appear on the show.

It just so happened that, during the same weekend, *Reel Injun* was scheduled to screen at Lightbox, part of a year of Truth and Reconciliation programming at TIFF's Cinematheque I'd planned to coincide with Canada's sesquicentennial. Afterward there was to be a panel discussion on the evolution of Indigenous-made media that featured Blackfoot filmmaker Cowboy Smithx, Anishinaabe comedian, writer, and podcast host Ryan McMahon, Cree filmmaker and cultural worker Ariel Smith, who was then running imagineNative, and me. That coming together would turn out to be a crucial source of catharsis and support. A religious or superstitious person might say that the timing was somehow preordained. Perhaps the ancestors *were* looking out for me that week, positioning me in the place they thought I could be most useful, with the strength and encouragement I would need to do what's right. I like to think that anyway.

When I reached out to tell the panellists about the TV appearance, Cowboy said he'd never seen the CBC broadcast centre and that he'd love to come along. I jumped at the idea. Not only was I grateful for the emotional support, but I also thought it would be kind of funny to show up with such a sizable backup. Six-foot-six with long dark hair, Cowboy can be an intimidating guy until you get to know him.

The morning of the appearance, I decided to wear my best suit. I've found that dressing nicely disarms those who wish to look down on Indigenous people. They so often think of us as poor or dirty or drunk. Turning up in a custom-made suit and shirt signals that the discourse will be one between equals—intellectual, financial, and otherwise. For a person relying on a power imbalance to cover the holes in their argument, that visual cue alone can break their spirit. I was going to look sharp while making Kay look foolish.

When Cowboy and I arrived, the show's producers took us upstairs to the studio. Only as we rode up in the elevator did they inform me that Kay and I wouldn't be sitting at the same table for the segment. I'd be next to the host, Carole MacNeil, while he'd be at a separate table just off set and would appear on an inset screen. And despite both of us being physically present for this "debate," we also weren't introduced to each other before going on air. It was a bizarre setup and I still don't know the reasoning behind it.

Nor do I remember the specifics of most of what Kay said. He spent the bulk of his time minimizing his own involvement in the Twitter controversy and scrambling to pick up the pieces of the argument he was ostensibly there to make. One moment has remained with me, though. After framing his fellow media power brokers' attempts to fund an Appropriation Prize as a good thing because the backlash would raise further awareness around the need for diversity and inclusion—gee, thanks—Kay said, "I'd like to commend Jesse, who has conducted himself extremely graciously on social media. Not everybody has done so—on both sides of the argument—and I think a little more civility would do everyone good."

The disingenuous demand for "civil" discourse is a rhetorical tactic the privileged often employ in their attempts to dismiss the arguments of other communities before ever even engaging with them. It seeks to elevate tone over substance, and it suggests that the concerns of those who don't sound acceptable can simply be dismissed—along with the people themselves. In commending me for my supposed graciousness, Kay was asserting himself as the arbiter of decorum, as the judge with the power to decide who gets to state their case and how. In Twitter shorthand, this is known as "tone policing": an attempt to invalidate an argument because it's made with emotion. Of course it's easy to tone-police a discussion of cultural appropriation if you yourself have never been affected by it; of course it's easy to turn the pain and passion of someone whose life is threatened by police brutality against them if your own life is protected; of course it's easy to remain calm when you have nothing at risk.

Cultural appropriation is an emotional issue for Indigenous peoples. We forever live in its shadow and feel its effects. The absence of our voices has made it easy for inequality to persist, leaving many communities without the basic requirements for human survival while our stories are marketed and sold by others, our designs co-opted for sale in glossy magazines and discount racks alike. If we had more of a voice, that travesty would not have been allowed to stand; it would have been recognized, exposed, and acted on long ago. Even in the present moment, cultural appropriation steals the fundamentals of life from us. To have to argue that it even exists is an added indignity, especially given that the argument has to be made again and again and again. And yet any display of emotion can be labelled as irrationality, held up as proof of the weakness of our arguments as opposed to the fact of our humanity. When Kay "complimented" me, he was lauding a suppression of my very humanity—one possible only because I understood that I was arguing with Indigenous lives at stake. There would be no such suppression on that afternoon's Cinematheque panel.

I was already drained from the day. The CBC appearance had gone as planned, but there was still an emotional crash in its wake. Even if you've got a lot of experience doing live broadcasts, it can still be really intense, a huge adrenalin rush—especially when the subject actually means something to you. So when I took my place on stage at Cinematheque that night, knowing that the issue would come up, I felt unsure whether I had the energy left to properly discuss it. But when it did arise my fellow panellists imbued me with that strength. It was an emotional conversation; I'm sure I cried. As I've always found, though, the support among the Indigenous panellists was deep and truly felt. Later, we went out for dinner to celebrate, commiserate, and discuss the future. We drank, we ate, we disturbed the table next to ours—it was a needed infusion of joy.

At some point during the meal I got a call from a friend who told me Kay had resigned his position as editor of *The Walrus*, news that had not yet been made public. I didn't quite know how to take that information. Subsequent statements would downplay the role the Appropriation Prize fallout had in the decision, though the timing was difficult to overlook. If they'd wanted to make a real statement, the magazine's publishers could have replaced Kay with an Indigenous editor. They didn't, but since his departure *The Walrus* has shifted its editorial stance in a more inclusive direction. It's up to you to decide whether those two things are related.

I went home that night eager to get some sleep and looking forward to Sunday, which was Mother's Day. I'd made plans for the kids and me to celebrate Julie and my own mom, and I knew that time with them would be deeply restorative, reminding me of the good in the world. A big breakfast was a given, although not particularly unusual for a Sunday in our house, our favourite meal being anything likely to involve the presence of bacon. It was a special treat to have my mom there, though, and we laughed and ate freely, with no table next to us to disturb.

After breakfast and gift-giving I went up to our bedroom to get changed, which is when I noticed a flurry of notifications on my phone. Barbara Kay, who is Jonathan Kay's mother and herself a long-time columnist, had felt compelled to tweet something directed at me and her son in response to the TV segment. "TRC did not allow witnessing from anyone w positive #residentialschools experience," she wrote. "Would u give them platform?"

This statement was something she'd repeated many times, despite its being demonstrably untrue: the Truth and Reconciliation Commission report contains an entire section about the "positive" experience some had at residential schools. But that didn't stop Kay from doubling down, creating a thread full of denial while also admitting that she'd never read the report herself.

I knew what Kay the Elder was doing, of course: she was attempting to defend her son, a grown man who'd made his own decisions and comments, ones that may have cost him his job. She was also trying to swipe at a person she may have thought contributed to her son's new employment status. She was a mother trying to hurt someone for a perceived hurt done to her family.

It was a clumsy, even stupid, attack. Sadly, I've been subjected to enough of those in the past decade to have developed some armour against them. But it's always been a struggle for me to protect myself and my emotions around the subject of residential schools because of the trauma my own family suffered at the hands of those institutions and my firsthand knowledge of how the effects of that trauma have impacted our family through the generations. Standing in my bedroom thinking of my grandmother while reading a tweet that essentially denied the pain she'd experienced, I broke. I broke down, too, weeping silently so that my family wouldn't hear while I tried to compose myself enough to face them. But the fracture I felt was more than a loss of composure. Kay's tweet was getting responses supporting her. All I could think of was my grandmother, as a six-year-old, being hurt in that school because she was Ojibwe. I lay down and cried, not sure I'd be able to get back up. I could hear my family downstairs, talking and laughing. Eventually the worst of it passed. I got up and got dressed, but I still didn't trust myself to go downstairs, worried I would overwhelm my children with the pain I felt. I sat on the edge of the bed. After a while Julie came upstairs to find out what was taking so long and saw me deeply upset. She hugged me and asked what was wrong. I told her and she hugged me closer. She told me to pay no attention, to put the phone away, and to enjoy the day.

I tried, and failed. I responded to Kay's tweet, saying how upset I was. After that I did manage to put away my phone, but I couldn't stop stewing, visions of my grandmother in my head, which is what I was doing when a producer at *Metro Morning* called to ask if I'd come in early that week—Monday instead of my usual Tuesday slot—and address the Appropriation Prize issue in my column. I agreed, because I felt I had more to say, but when it came time to write the script later that afternoon, I couldn't. I managed a shoddy introduction and then just stared at the blinking cursor.

I sat in front of that screen for hours. I wrote many things but erased them all. The words I could find weren't angry enough, clear enough, precise enough, emotional enough to convey what was happening inside me, to fully capture what I wanted to say. At about nine that night I threw in the towel. I sent an email to the show's overnight producer, Ron McKeen, who was usually the one who received my scripts. I told him I just couldn't get anything down, but that it would all work out on the air; I asked that Matt Galloway, the show's host, deliver an intro and said that he and I would take it from there. It was the first time in twenty years as a columnist that I hadn't turned in a written script. It felt like a failure, but I didn't know what else to do. I was drained from the emotion of the weekend, and I needed to at least get enough sleep to wake up ready to perform on the air. I asked that they trust me to find the words when they were needed. I'm still so grateful that they agreed.

That column would be the most emotional experience I've ever had on the air. I wrote above that cultural appropriation is a difficult, affecting subject for many Indigenous people to discuss, something that is certainly the case for me. There are many reasons for that, some of which I've already outlined—the exhausting process of taking up the same argument again and again, the pain of having to argue for your own humanity, the near-impossible self-control required to speak on these issues while remaining "gracious" enough to be listened to at all—but the central one, in my view, is that it taps you into a river of grief, despair, and suffering that stretches back for generations.

White people asserting their right to take our stories, to describe our lives without understanding them, to misrepresent us, is nothing new. The first films ever made in the United States, shot by Thomas Edison in 1894, were of Indigenous people. These recordings were presented to their white audiences as documentary footage, a tantalizing glimpse at real-life Indians, but they actually featured performers from *Buffalo Bill's Wild West* show. As if that lie weren't enough of a travesty, the Religious Crimes Code of 1883 made the dances that Edison captured, which could've correctly been billed as "traditional" or "ceremonial," illegal for Sioux to perform in their own communities. In Canada a similar piece of legislation, the 1885 potlatch ban, had begun by outlawing a ceremony specific to some west coast nations before extending eastward to take in the sun dance and any other Indigenous ceremony or gathering that could be deemed a threat to assimilationist efforts. In other words, the two settler states displayed a common approach to Indigenous ceremony and storytelling. Indigenous people could do these dances for a white audience or a white director and his white camera, but if performed in the proper cultural context, the dancers would face jail time or worse.

Marketing Indigenous performance as Indigenous existence in this way allowed white intermediaries to shape the popular conception of Indigenous life and identity, and rarely to our benefit. The 1922 film *Nanook of the North*, which claims to depict the lives of Inuit living in northern Quebec, is another such project. Often billed as "the first documentary," the whole thing's made up. Everything shown on screen is a constructed reality. Swapping the truth of Indigenous life for a colonizer's invented interpretation creates the gap in understanding that has so long framed First Nations, Métis, and Inuit peoples as primitive and inferior. That depiction of us and our communities has in turn been used as justification for policies and practices that treated us as something less than full human beings. The harm done is immeasurable.

The potlatch ban endured until 1951—meaning that for sixty-six years it was illegal for Indigenous peoples in Canada to engage in pretty much any cultural practice that wasn't imposed on them by settlers. Of course, many nations maintained their cultural practices in secret, often through daring and ingenious means, but there was no way of completely escaping the enormous damage wrought on our communities, the attack on our history and way of life. When I think of the sheer volume of knowledge lost, of stories that will never again be told, it makes me despair. That feeling is compounded when I think of what we got in place of what was taken.

Under the ban it was also deemed unnecessary for cultural items used in ceremony to be held by the communities that created them. They couldn't use them anymore, so why did they need them at all? Instead, during this period many of these sacred items were seized and placed in museums and galleries around the world. Of course, those institutions didn't employ Indigenous people from the nations they robbed—most still don't—so they relied on white curators to contextualize the sacred items for their white audiences. This is the face of cultural appropriation in Canada: forcibly preventing Indigenous communities from engaging in their cultural practices, telling their stories, and using their ceremonial items so that white people can recontextualize and misconstrue them for profit.

And it's not just the actions of our major cultural institutions that are appropriationist; appropriation is *the central ethos that shaped them.*

Many of these organizations and institutions were founded during this same period: the Canadian Museum of History was founded in 1856, the National Gallery of Canada in 1880, the Art Museum of Toronto (now the Art Gallery of Ontario) in 1900, the Royal Ontario Museum in 1912, the CBC in 1936, the National Film Board in 1939—it goes on. These institutions were born not simply excusing appropriation, dismissing it, or reducing it to a pedantic argument as they do today; they were born with cultural appropriation as the law. It infused their every action, their every engagement with Indigenous culture, the very way they thought of Indigenous people when they thought of us at all.

Any argument that today seeks to frame cultural appropriation as an invention designed to limit free speech (with the invention tacitly understood to be BIPOC's and the speech tacitly understood to be white) ignores this history entirely. It also ignores the ways this history has built and informed the modern day. That the Twitter pile-on of elite media executives was entirely white is unsurprising: with appropriation and white supremacy baked into their very cores, mainstream media and cultural institutions remain next to impossible for BIPOC to enter and ascend. That lack of representation means our stories are still being told almost exclusively through a white lens or being otherwise overlooked, and that lack has meant dire consequences for us. At the time of the calls to fund an Appropriation Prize, my home community, Serpent River, had been on a boil water advisory off and on for fifteen years. If we had more voices in the media to tell our stories, to advocate for our humanity, it's hard to imagine something so fundamental being denied us for so long. If the executives who participated in that call, and others like them, had hired some Indigenous writers, editors, producers, and broadcasters instead of playing around on their phones, the epidemic of missing and murdered Indigenous women might have been covered with the urgency necessary to inspire meaningful action. For Indigenous people, cultural appropriation isn't just a matter of representation and responsible storytelling; it is life and death. If the emotion it inspires didn't make sense to you before, I hope it does now.

In the *Metro Morning* studio, Matt Galloway delivered the introduction that the producer had written. After quickly recapping Niedzviecki's editorial, the backlash, the Appropriation Prize, the next round of backlash, my "debate" with Kay, and his resignation, it ended with a question. "What have the last few days been like for you?" Matt asked.

In my chair across the table from him, I took a second or two to collect myself before answering. I was exhausted, frankly, wrung out. The little sleep I'd managed hadn't been enough to fully recover from the way I'd felt staring at that blinking cursor the night before: as though I'd run out of words, as though I'd already argued for the value of our lives every way I could possibly think to and it still hadn't been enough. I was furious and spent.

I still had only a sense of what I would say, some quick notes on a handful of sheets of paper spread in front of me, but I'd known all along that when I needed them, the words would come. What I hadn't expected was that my *nookomis* would come, too. There in the studio I felt her beside me, a physical presence as strong as if she'd walked through the door and laid a hand on my shoulder, and I heard her voice, whispering to me with that rez accent and the distinctive turns of phrase unique to her and the people who come from where we come from. Strength, belief, and reassurance radiated from her—the strength to say this all yet again, the belief that this time it might finally be heard, the reassurance that no matter what happened, as long as I spoke the truth, everything would turn out all right.

So, I did. I reminded Canadians that appropriation is the foundation on which our country is built, and that it's not just cultural appropriation but appropriation of all things Indigenous—our lives, our land. I asked them to reconsider the voices we've centred for so long, and to take note of how ill-equipped the media establishment was to participate in any effort to help this country recreate itself and move past its worst colonial tendencies. I asked them to disregard the false championing of free speech and instead acknowledge that true freedom of speech isn't free, that it comes with responsibilities. And I let it be known that words and apologies were fine, but the time had come for action:

"These things can't happen again," I said that morning. "This absorbs so much energy, it causes so much pain in our communities. To have to re-argue for our value as human beings? On our own land? In a foreign language, as I do to you now—one imposed on us? Please. What are we talking about in 2017? I'm sorry."

I'd never wanted to cry on the air, but I was powerless to prevent myself. I'd poured all my frustration and anger, my hope and strength into those words, and had spoken from my heart and soul. I'd given so much that I had nothing left to hold back the tears. I just gave in to them.

When the interview finished, Matt and I embraced outside the studio. We'd been in touch over the weekend leading up to my appearance, and in those conversations he'd told me, "You're going to say what you need to say. You just do it. I won't interrupt." He'd been true to his word. As we said our goodbyes, with an intensity we wouldn't approach again until he left *Metro Morning*, he told me I'd done a great job and thanked me.

As hard as the column had been, I left to get my usual breakfast feeling that I'd said what needed to be said in the exact way I'd wanted to say it. The column would go viral almost immediately, and when I finally got around to checking my messages and social media feeds, I saw the impact it was having. It remains the most widely viewed and shared piece of work I've ever produced. It's also almost certainly the reason this book exists, since mixed in with the messages of support were notes from a handful of publishers. There were also, perhaps inevitably, many hateful words and a couple of death threats.

***

Since that May weekend, cultural appropriation hasn't left the field of discussion in Canada. Awareness of it as an issue—and as a debate perhaps best avoided—is at an all-time high, and there are signs, albeit nascent ones, of actual change. The Canada Council for the Arts released a statement denouncing appropriation, and more effort is being made across the board to ensure that communities represented in art are also those who make the art. In the future, I hope they'll also be engaged in decisions about who receives financial support for their work.

Many Canadians have reached out to me, hoping to discuss cultural appropriation. These conversations often feel fruitful, and people's desire to have them is usually encouraging, but being asked to retread the same ground again and again—in speeches, direct messages, and emails, on panels and planes, at dinner parties and work lunches—is exhausting, even when the requests come from the well-intentioned. And, to be honest, I don't think cultural appropriation is all that interesting a subject: it's not the adding of something but the removal, the subtraction, the negative. And it's not even *our* thing. Cultural appropriation is Canada's tactic, a colonizer's tool. Indigenous people didn't invent it; we just suffer its consequences—so why should we have to endlessly explain it?

At some point I decided to instead talk about the issue from the other side. Rather than explain all the ways cultures are attacked, robbed, and dismantled, I now outline how they're defended and supported—I focus on the positive, on the creative act. And I do that by discussing narrative sovereignty.

Narrative sovereignty is the idea that people, communities, and nations should control their own stories and the tools used in that storytelling. On an individual level, it looks something like this: If I'm to tell you a story, I decide what story to tell, how to tell it, and where to tell it, and I'm protected from your then turning around and telling your version of the same story for profit without asking my permission or acknowledging that you heard it from me. Of course, the whole thing gets more complicated with collaborative mediums like film and television, but not so complicated that the Canadian government didn't long ago figure out and implement a system for protecting its own narrative sovereignty.

For example, in this country, the screen sector is heavily funded and meticulously presided over by government bodies. To receive their support, a production needs to prove that it's Canadian. That identity can be judged according to a variety of measures, but the national origins of a project's creative decision makers and key financial backers are a crucial factor, with the content itself being of secondary importance. In short, if the people telling it are Canadian, it's a Canadian story. This is how a story that reaches beyond our borders can still be counted. Conversely, if the film is about Canada but Canadians aren't the ones telling the story, it's not a Canadian film.

When you look at the history of film, visual art, music, and literature in this country and apply these same criteria to depictions of Indigenous life, it becomes immediately obvious that First Nations, Métis, and Inuit narrative sovereignty has rarely been a consideration. The hypocrisy of that, given the Canadian government's rabid defence of its own stories, is an intentional one, because our stories are a threat to the one Canada tells itself and the world.

This country is a colonial settler state. Its origins lie in a massive resource extraction project—the exploitation of the land's natural bounty in order to enrich Europeans—that was often both illegal and murderous. In order to justify all that selfishness, greed, and violence, Canada used storytelling to craft an alternative history and identity. In this version, settlers arrived to find no "real" people here, only primitive groups situated somewhere between human and animal. It nevertheless dealt with these groups humanely, purchasing their land fair and square, elevating their societies toward a European ideal, educating their children, and just generally doing anything it could think of to help them become Canadians.

This is the story Canada can live with, the one in which it did nothing wrong and everything right, the one in which it remains, to this day, a nation of immense natural beauty and overwhelming politeness. It's not the story Indigenous people tell, of course, because we tell the truth. We are simply not given the space to speak.

This is also why so many Canadians have grown up knowing so little of Indigenous life. In all my time travelling and speaking across this land, it's one of the most consistent responses my talks elicit: "I just didn't know."

It's purposeful that you don't know—and not just about recent horrors, among them residential schools and the epidemic of missing and murdered women and girls, but also the history of this place before it was ever Canada, before anyone with ideas of Canada ever lived here. That story has been around far longer than any of the ones Canada tells. And yet, as I noted earlier, back when I was in high school at Crescent the emphasis was on how European countries made treaties with each other, not on how treaties between settler nations and Indigenous peoples allowed this country to come into existence. We must see this as an exercise in narrative sovereignty.

But for all of Canada's territorial instincts and actions around the stories told here, in its denials of a proper voice for Indigenous peoples it has ruined any chance at telling its own story truthfully and completely. Indigenous communities are as crucial to the story of this place as their English and French counterparts, so in attacking the narrative sovereignty of First Nations, Métis, and Inuit peoples Canada has torn a hole in itself. That absence is the root of this nation's ongoing identity crisis. As it attempts to fill the void with hockey, Tim Hortons, and jean jackets, it ignores the truth that what has been and remains missing from Canadian culture are the stories of Indigenous peoples, the stories that have been told on this land for thousands of years.

Embracing these stories, embracing the people behind them, their history, their nations, and yes, even their sovereignty, is where Canada's true identity lies. It's also where we'll find this country's true potential: in the vision our ancestors had for it, which was as a multinational place where First Nations, Inuit, Métis, and newcomers shared the land, respected each other, and were allowed to live as they wanted. In this telling, Canada would be formed not by laws passed in foreign lands but by the relationships that bound it together.

Indigenous sovereignty—narrative, political, and physical—poses a threat only to the systems in this country we should be trying to rid ourselves of. Supporting that sovereignty is the pathway to Canada truly becoming the kind of world leader it has always wanted, and claimed, to be.

Cultural appropriation is an act of immaturity. Canada needs to grow out of it.

CHAPTER 14

The Director's Chair

A month and a day after the Appropriation Prize's impromptu fundraiser, a very different type of Canadian media initiative was officially launched. Speaking at the Banff World Media Festival on June 12, 2017, Melanie Joly, then federal heritage minister, announced the formation of the Indigenous Screen Office (ISO)—an organization intended to support the creation, distribution, and marketing of Indigenous content. "Too often, Indigenous creators have faced systematic barriers in the industry that have made it difficult to share their stories," Joly said during the announcement. The ISO, she went on, would "help address these barriers, provide direct support to creators, and showcase Indigenous content in Canada and on the world stage." It also came with a powerful group of backers: the Aboriginal Peoples Television Network (APTN), the CBC, the Canada Media Fund (CMF), Telefilm Canada, the Canadian Media Producers Association (CMPA), and the National Film Board of Canada.

The ISO was a direct result of a report on the future of Indigenous screen production in Canada authored by Indigenous governance consultant Marcia Nickerson—the latest in a long line of documents to identify the systemic issues faced by First Nations, Métis, and Inuit people in Canada's media sector. Released in 2016, the report built on advocacy for the establishment of an organization like the ISO that had been going on for more than two decades, beginning shortly after Screen Australia founded its Indigenous Department in 1993.

I'd gotten involved with that advocacy effort while Nickerson was writing her report. At the time, despite the obvious need there were no dedicated supports for Indigenous artists. The idea had always been that any Indian who wanted to make a movie would go through either the French or English side of organizations like Telefilm and the NFB, same as everyone else. As a result, few Indians made movies—if there was an Indigenous story, it was undoubtedly made by a non-Indigenous production team. So to see the calls for addressing that inequity finally answered with the funding of the ISO was a watershed moment for Indigenous creators in Canada. If there were an opposite of the Appropriation Prize, this was it.

There's never a bad time for such excellent news, but there *are* particularly good ones. When the ISO came along I was in dire need of reasons to be hopeful about Canadian media. The awful taste of the Appropriation Prize was still in my mouth—in part because people kept asking me to talk about it—and I was also in the midst of that slide into tokenism I talked about earlier, the one that would ultimately turn my dream job into a nightmare and end with my resignation from TIFF. So seeing years of advocacy work manifest in something tangible was a crucial shot in the arm. But before I knew it, the ISO would be a lot more to me than an outside source of inspiration.

When the film festival began in early September 2017 I knew I'd be officially leaving TIFF at the end of it; although I'd submitted my letter of resignation, I'd kept that news from even my close friends in the industry. I had no idea what the future held for me. Still, I'd decided to just enjoy the festival and then start figuring things out once the craziest two weeks in Canadian film were over.

That year one of the festival's early events, co-hosted with Telefilm, was a breakfast for the Indigenous filmmakers whose work had been selected. Held at a rooftop space on a beautiful late-summer day, here were gathered artists whose work I deeply admired, celebrating a major achievement in their careers alongside many people who'd championed them. There was a collective feeling of having finally made it, and of having done so in the face of a system that didn't want to see us succeed. With all that in the air, it wasn't hard to have a good time.

At some point during the festivities I was approached by Marcia Nickerson, who's an old friend, and Valerie Creighton, the head of the CMF. They asked to speak privately, so we found a place away from the hubbub to talk. The first order of business for the groups who'd chipped in funding for the ISO was to find and hire its first director, someone to create a plan for building the office from the ground up while also advocating for the funds needed to do so. In the months since the announcement I'd been approached to gauge my interest, but had resisted the idea, still convinced I'd find a way to make things work at TIFF. Now, though, my life and career looked vastly different—and here were Nickerson and Creighton pushing me to apply.

My time at TIFF had been fun, engaging, enraging at times, and completely life-changing. I'd learned so much about how the movie business actually worked. But having seen behind the curtain, I didn't feel I could go back to a seat in the audience; if I were going to stick around movies, my lifelong love, then it would have to be in a new capacity. Actually *making* a film was a possibility I'd never been able to dismiss, but I believed that the Indigenous Screen Office could be a real change agent within the Canadian sector—and, in fact, the global arena. Here was an opportunity—especially with the reconciliation-happy Trudeau Liberals in office—to truly open up space for Indigenous storytellers and stories. And I've always believed that those stories, and the people and communities from which they spring, are key to any hope Canada has of fulfilling its promise as a nation.

In building the ISO from the ground up, I'd have the chance to create an institution where Indigenous people were always centred, one that worked to make changes in the present with an eye toward what those changes would mean in the years to come. It was a chance to shed the feeling of being a token while simultaneously working to make it harder for us to be tokenized, to be dehumanized, in the first place. It was a chance to help my community embrace a new era of storytelling and, perhaps, change Canada along the way. And it was a chance to take concrete steps toward a goal I'd long emphasized: getting more Indigenous people into the media industry, creating as much leeway as possible for the young First Nations, Métis, and Inuit people who will truly have the vision necessary to shape the future.

It wasn't just time for us to have a seat at the table; it was time for us to build a table of our own. And I wanted to be part of the construction process. Later that year I applied for the role, and in late January 2018 I was officially announced as the first director of the Indigenous Screen Office.

The best art comes when artists are the most free to just do their thing unimpeded by systems and rules. It follows, then, that the best filmmakers are the ones who manage to carve out a space in which they can create without studios, production companies, and funding bodies interfering. In Hollywood, securing that freedom has been a particular challenge from the very beginning, even for many established white male directors. But the filmmakers we idolize are often those who found that room to pursue their true vision and work unencumbered.

Consider Stanley Kubrick. I've spent more time with his films than any other director's in the history of cinema, and the fight for that freedom, along with the fruits of unlocking it, basically sums up his story. As an accomplished but still emerging director he was hired to take over a troubled mega-production in *Spartacus*, whose subsequent success turned him into an industry darling. Yet after he made *Lolita* he rejected

Hollywood's controlling ways, moving to England and remaining there for the rest of his life, rarely making trips back and avoiding the type of studio oversight his colleagues endured.

Voilà. The guy made thirteen movies; they're all amazing; none of them are the same. And because he was one of the last directors to have final-cut privileges, there's barely been anyone like him since.

It's artists with the freedom that Kubrick ultimately enjoyed who make the biggest impact on society, the ones who figure out how to be themselves within systems that constantly pressure them to be someone else. They're the ones who give us these amazing artifacts, experiences, and stories that people will still be talking about a hundred years from now. So, in taking the reins of the ISO, the first questions I asked myself were "How can I make sure Indigenous creators are able to carve out that same kind of space? How do I enable and empower as many Indigenous Kubricks as possible?"

Facilitating that kind of artistic freedom is a tricky proposition even when you're not focused on a historically marginalized, oppressed, and under-resourced community. For the artist, there's the task of finding their actual voice in the first place and then maintaining it, even defending it, from being diluted and swayed by outside forces. That's a journey in itself—one that requires them to resist popular trends and break away from the tropes, techniques, and influence of established artists. And if they manage all that, then they have to protect themselves from the big cultural and financial institutions that invariably try to tame individual expression and bend it into recognizable shapes, doing everything in their considerable power to prevent artists from having the type of freedom I'm talking about, despite the fact that they inevitably fawn over anyone who manages to achieve it. In short, it can be a frustrating, limiting, and paradoxical industry at the best of times.

And, obviously, Indigenous creators have almost never enjoyed the best of times, the best of anything. Instead they've experienced not only a historical lack of financial and institutional support but also a cultural system largely devoid of Indigenous presence. When the ISO was announced, Telefilm, the CMF, and the NFB had three Indigenous employees spread between them, none of whom were in any position of power or authority—and the number still doesn't reach double digits. Though cultural gatekeepers have shown a healthy appetite for Indigenous stories—one that has only grown in recent years—their preference, intentional or otherwise, has always been to see those stories filtered through white artists and their white lenses. I've already outlined how the colonizer's will to appropriate rather than recognize Indigenous humanity forms the very foundation of most major cultural institutions. That history still manifests today in the neglect and exclusion of Indigenous artists, as it did in 2017 and 1985 and 1953 and 1937, as it will forever unless fundamental change is made. Before it's possible to win true artistic freedom for First Nations, Métis, and Inuit creators within these systems, then, you've got to get them over the walls and through the door. But that process also has to be one that fights for vitally necessary fundamental change in the industry itself. If it doesn't, all that effort serves only to funnel Indigenous artists into places that don't really want them or their work, that limit what they're able to create, and that make them miserable.

So, for the ISO to succeed in its mission, it had to be an entirely new type of Canadian cultural institution, one that didn't replicate the prejudices and failures of its colonial counterparts. That is, of course, no small undertaking, and it wasn't made much easier by the fact that I was setting out alone. In the grand tradition of projects in Indian country, which are almost always funded just below the sustainable level, funded to fail in many ways, the amount committed to found the ISO was just $235,000—not enough to rent an office or hire any staff. In addition to my advocacy on behalf of Indigenous creators, then, I had to advocate for the continued existence of the ISO itself while trying to imagine what that existence would look like.

I began where you might expect: with narrative sovereignty. Indigenous communities have had enough experience with outsiders telling them how to tell their stories and governing bodies attempting to define what constitutes an Indigenous person, an Indigenous artist, Indigenous land, Indigenous anything. Though often (conveniently) framed as attempts to "help," efforts that take a prescriptive tack not only fail Indigenous communities but often harm them. I knew the ISO could never try to define Indigenous content for everyone; I don't think it's my place to tell even someone from Serpent River, a community I belong to, that "this is how you must do things." Any organization looking to truly support First Nations, Métis, and Inuit storytelling has to avoid being prescriptive in any part of its approach. The purpose of the ISO's existence, then, is to listen to the wants and needs of Indigenous content creators and their communities and then help build the tools that allow them to achieve those goals on their own, any way they see fit. We're here to offer something to Indigenous communities, not to demand anything of them. Other than the single parameter that Indigenous content can't be created by non-Indigenous people, why limit things?

Though "screen" is right in the name of the office, I don't even want us to be prescriptive about the medium through which artists choose to express themselves. What we're trying to build is something broader than that, something storytelling-based—full stop. As a result, our goals are also suitably broad. We advocate for increased representation in all aspects of the media business; we seek narrative sovereignty and autonomy for Indigenous people within the industry's existing structures; and we try to establish economic connections between the content sector and Indigenous communities in the hope of encouraging financial opportunities for those communities that wouldn't otherwise exist.

For communities seeking economic independence, increased exposure to movie and television production offers a possible way to make money that doesn't pull people away from their families, traditions, and land and that doesn't exact the kind of environmental toll nations are almost always asked to stomach in order to survive.

The state has always wanted to keep Indigenous people dependent on the exploitation of natural resources for survival. That's why Canada has no urban reserves, no reserves anywhere near economic centres. When we were forcibly relocated it was to the least desirable land in the least desirable places. And when we got there we were legally prevented from hiring lawyers, from gathering in groups, from engaging in any activity that might've allowed us to organize resistance to colonial powers' plundering and pillaging of all that once belonged to us. And whenever the government's greed exhausted the land they'd already taken, they simply cast an acquiring eye over treaty territory. They ignored their own laws to take what they wanted again and again, and when the threat of force didn't sway us, they used force itself—all the while disguising their crimes by inventing an alternative history, by banning us from telling the truth, by framing the consultation process and community decisions around pipeline projects and other resource extraction projects as matters of free will, free markets, and free choice.

Imagine a city planner coming to your door one day and informing you of a proposal to build a subway under the house you live in with your family, your children. "You can stay and endure the rumbling or we can buy your house at half its sale price," the planner says. That's the sum total of your choice; the part that isn't changing is the subway going through. Would that feel to you like a matter of free will, or just the free market?

Indigenous communities are never presented with the choice to just say no. Instead, the choice is always either to benefit from the pipeline or not to benefit from it. There are those who bravely stand up and pro-test the choice itself—the absence of choice. Many communities, though, don't have the wherewithal for that fight and don't see any other opportunities on the horizon. They say yes because it's really the only available option. Any other group of people would do the same thing.

Again, this lack of choice is no accident. Limiting economic and educational opportunities in Indigenous communities is a means of driving people out of those communities, off the land, in search of a better, more stable life. Even efforts to address inequalities of opportunity mostly involve physically or emotionally distancing Indigenous people from their homes. Scholarships like the one I received to go to university, for example, still pull people out of their communities to attend school. And if they don't do that they create arguments, jealousies, and resentments about who got what piece of a pie that's never big enough to address the true need.

Projects aimed at improving the quality of Indigenous life without requiring that life to take place off-rez or that improvement to come at a steep environmental and ethical price are few and far between and almost always created and run by Indigenous communities themselves. That these projects are also chronically underfunded is obviously no surprise. That they can teach us so much about the most effective ways to truly support First Nations, Métis, and Inuit communities shouldn't be a surprise either. Nor should the fact that so many of those lessons reinforce the importance of sovereignty—not only narrative sovereignty, but freedom and power of choice in all things relating to their own nations.

To that end, one of the ISO's goals is to eventually have staff across Turtle Island. Again, we're trying to avoid replicating the harm caused by colonial models of organization, and that includes the idea that a land mass as large as Canada and as disparate in its population can be properly managed by a centralized government. As I often like to say, Canada has been diverse forever; the many different First Nations across the land could have formed a single, overarching government if we'd thought it was smart. We didn't, and it's not as though we simply avoided the choice or never encountered one another and talked it through. There is recorded history of multinational meetings in which we all sat down and discussed it. Instead what we came up with were things like the 1764 Treaty of Fort Niagara, which outlined a very different relationship to the Crown and its governing structures from the one we have now. In the case of the ISO, a centralized operation that doesn't allow an Inuit artist to talk to a fellow Inuk when interacting with the office would miss the point.

None of these are new ideas, but the ISO does offer one of the best opportunities to apply them practically and on a national scale. It took years of advocacy work to create this chance, but rather than dwell on that effort or be discouraged by the lag between need and response, I try to focus on the present. There's a reason it's happening now; there's something about this moment—the TRC, the government in power, the gradual and hard-won breakthrough of Indigenous artists into the popular consciousness, the amplification of our voices through social media—that coalesced and allowed the ISO to become a reality at all. And its existence is a particularly significant achievement in the screen sector, which will always lag behind other areas of creative expression simply because of its scale, the fact that it's an industry as well as an art form. To make a movie or TV show requires a lot more upfront resources than the writing of a novel, the painting of a picture. You need many more people on your side to make any progress, and they have to be willing to put their money behind you. But we've cleared even that hurdle, and the fact that there's still so much work to be done shouldn't take away from the hope and possibility that mark such a crucial juncture.

I've always believed that since colonization is largely a destructive process—an extraction that gives nothing back—one of the simplest ways to decolonize is to create. Given the tools to tell their own stories the way they want, and to market and sell those stories, Indigenous communities can generate economic opportunity where currently none exists, without in the process taking anything from the land beyond the room to think. They can reshape our perception of what Canada can be. And they can do so not only by reimagining the relationship between the Canadian government and Indigenous peoples, though that reimagining is desperately needed, but also by introducing new possibilities for our relationships with nature, family, community, spirituality, and ourselves.

The relative cost of something so beneficial to Canadian life is peanuts, too. Ahead of the 2020 federal budget, the ISO asked for $27 million annually to support Indigenous storytelling—a figure dwarfed by the billions Canada currently spends each year on its own narrative sovereignty through mechanisms like Telefilm, the CBC, and the Canada Council for the Arts. Even within the current legislative construct, then, our ask is a modest one. If we were to get equitable placement within the Broadcasting Act, a much larger pool of money would be involved. And that ask is made all the more modest when you consider how unfair the current construct is for Indigenous people, how divorced from the reality of what's been done to us.

When the COVID-19 pandemic ended up postponing that 2020 federal budget, the ISO's request for funding couldn't be granted. And yet the introduction of proposed amendments to the Broadcasting Act inspires some hope. Those amendments drop a particularly nagging piece of language put in place back in 1993—the last time the Act was revised—according to which the Canadian broadcasting sector should support Aboriginal broadcasts "when funds are available." I can't speak to the intent of this language, but I can relate the result, which is that funds didn't become available until very recently. Other than the founding of APTN in 1999, there has never been substantial investment in Indigenous screen stories. The removal of that qualifier from the Act means that Indigenous content will become a required element of the Canadian broadcast landscape, just as French and English content are. That should mean new investment to support that requirement. As of this writing the bill awaits passage, but in a year freighted with pessimism its introduction was an optimistic moment.

It's hyperbolic but not inaccurate to say that the entirety of the Canadian government's budget is based on the proceeds of an ongoing crime, one committed against Indigenous communities. And even in the colonial social system you don't get to keep the proceeds of a crime. It is my view, then, that all that money carries an obligation. If you're a telecom company running your cables across Indigenous land, I don't care what treaty—or imagined treaty—said you can do that and I don't care that you paid for the infrastructure; you're still profiting off the illegal seizure of Indigenous land. In fact, there is no business, no economic venture, in this country that could exist or continue to function without access to Indigenous land and resources.

Now, I won't go so far as to suggest that *all* that money should be handed over to Indigenous people. Kicking our settler neighbours out of their homes, robbing them of their livelihoods: these wouldn't be immoral acts—we'd simply be doing what had been done to us, returning the favour—but they would be impractical and unnecessary ones. What I *am* suggesting is that Indigenous peoples should at least have a say in how the government spends money that couldn't exist without our land, and that our communities shouldn't ever suffer from the lack of such necessities as food, water, shelter, education, health care, family, and culture.

Crucial to having that say is having a real and meaningful voice, and crucial to establishing and encouraging that voice is reclaiming the right to tell our own stories. I sometimes sit and just try to imagine a Canada fifty years into the future, one in which five or ten times as much Indigenous-made content is created each year. I think about what that would do to the way the non-Indigenous population of Canada understands us, and what that understanding would do to the relationship between us and the rest of the country. So much of the violence and inequality we face comes from pure ignorance. Some of it is wilful, of course, but even then the solution is to spread the truth, to make the undeniable things undeniable for everyone.

When we don't have to waste time arguing about the undeniable facts of history, when we don't have to expend emotional energy defending the undeniable fact that we're human beings, when we don't have to sacrifice any more lives waiting for people to care about our missing and murdered women and girls—only then will we be able to move on to acting against these injustices. And I believe that the way to get to that mutual understanding begins with our stories, our narrative sovereignty.

So the goal isn't even the movies and TV shows themselves—they'll be excellent and needed, and despite the age-old excuses the industry has leaned on to avoid funding Indigenous productions, there *will* be an audience dying to see them. Instead the goal is the cumulative effect these narratives will have on the popular consciousness in this country; what they'll mean decades from now, after we're gone.

I hope they'll have helped to make this a changed place. I hope Indigenous communities won't need to barricade against pipelines, mines, and development projects because average Canadians will have already understood the issues and demanded better of their representatives. I hope police will no longer harass, brutalize, and murder us because they'll have finally seen us as human beings. I hope the ISO becomes fully operational and starts creating new worlds like a reverse Death Star.

I hope, because the alternative is that our voices remain silenced, the truth of this country's past and present remain unacknowledged, colonialism and capitalism continue unrestrained. Indigenous communities have already seen that future. It is one of crumbling social safety nets, mental health and addiction crises, economic depression, and environmental collapse. It is a future without hope. We know it because so many of us live it now. We can save you from it, Canada, but not if you refuse to listen.

CHAPTER 15

Unreconciled

If you've been awake in Canada in the last decade or so, you've come across the idea of "reconciliation" between this nation and the Indigenous ones that preceded it. Since the lead-up to the federal election of 2015, it's been a favourite word of Justin Trudeau's and his Liberal government. It began as a campaign slogan, a tool to help win an election that allowed Trudeau and his crowd to appear progressive while advancing the same colonial agenda that has fuelled Canada since its inception. It has continued to live in these politicians' mouths as a hollow promise to renew a "nation-to-nation" relationship.

The year Trudeau displaced Stephen Harper as prime minister was also the year the final report of the Truth and Reconciliation Commission was released. Created to expose the reality of the residential schools system and its ongoing legacy of pain and trauma, the TRC was a seven-year process that ultimately resulted in a series of "findings" that already existed in plain sight—that had been a matter of public record for at least twenty years, since the final report of the Royal Commission on

Aboriginal Peoples. Residential schools, the report stated, had been a tool of colonialism that inflicted physical, mental, and emotional damage on Indigenous people that has resonated for generations, that continues to be felt. Hardly a revelation.

The power of the TRC lay not in this discovery of facts already known to anyone who cared enough to look. No, the true power was in the process itself. Over those seven years, more than six thousand witnesses testified before the Commission, many of them survivors of residential schools. Many told their stories for the first time. Many of us heard those stories for the first time. That act of truth-telling was powerful and necessary.

And from that bravery came the TRC's ninety-four calls to action, meant to honour those stories and the people who lived them as well as all those who were never afforded the chance to tell their own. Taken together, these steps offer a path to reconciliation that is paint-by-numbers easy to wrap your head around: start at number one, proceed to ninety-four, and boom, there you have it—reconciled. But that apparent ease hasn't translated to implementation or action. More than half a decade since the report's release, only a scant few of the calls have been addressed, by even the most generous of interpretations. Some would say that the true number is zero.

The reason for that total, or near-total, inertia is simple, but it requires, first, the acknowledgment that "reconciliation" is the wrong word for both the situation and the goal. To reconcile in this context would be to repair a once functional relationship. No such thing has ever meaningfully existed between Indigenous nations and the state of Canada, so reconciliation is impossible here, as it is impossible in any colonial settler state. What is truly needed, then, is the building of a functional relationship in the first place; to stop pretending that the current relationship is worth saving and to discard it and start over. This is the process the TRC's ninety-four steps actually outline, and the simple reason why none of them has been undertaken is that Canada has no desire to build a functional relationship with Indigenous peoples; it exists for the exact opposite purpose.

As is the case with many colonial settler states, Canada was founded on the Doctrine of Discovery and the idea of *terra nullius*, nobody's land. In this case, the nobodies were First Nations and Inuit peoples. Yes, we'd been here for millennia when the Europeans arrived, but because we weren't white Christians, we just didn't count. Our presence was an absence of humanity. The land was there for the taking.

Canada's very being, then, is dependent on the assertion that Indigenous people are less than human. In other words, as long as we exist outside the confines of colonial history books and storytelling, we're a threat. And we're still here, still human beings who signify that Canada is nothing more than a murderous resource extraction project. After all, which nation seems more legitimate: one that evolved over thousands of years based on the land it still occupies or one that's less than two hundred years old and illegally occupying lands it stole on the basis of laws passed in countries across an ocean and reflecting the philosophy that any culture that differs from its own is inferior? Not exactly the Riemann hypothesis, is it?

In the face of this existential threat, you'd think the politicians in power wouldn't have adopted reconciliation as a buzzword. That they did is the first hint that the version of the idea they put forward isn't at all what the TRC outlines; it's just another way to circle the wagons in defence of capitalism and white supremacy. The state's version of reconciliation is one of empty apologies. It seeks to frame the crimes of colonialism as wrongs that exist only in the past, foisting any guilt or blame onto long-dead antagonists who can't answer for their actions. It refuses to acknowledge that colonialism persists, that there are those who still benefit from the subjugation of Indigenous communities. And in doing so it still denies Indigenous people our personhood. The relationship it outlines is not one of mutual understanding, reparations, and healing, but yet another one-sided resource extraction project. Just as we've been exploited in the name of oil, uranium, timber, gold, and a good story, we're also exploited for forgiveness, for the elimination of white guilt.

You'll notice that when colonial politicians espouse this version of reconciliation there's a crucial word they almost always leave out: truth. It's a word that has long been married to "reconciliation" precisely because they're inseparable, because no meaningful positive change can be made without an honest accounting. When someone speaks of reconciliation and doesn't mention truth, it's because they're not actually seeking a rebalancing of the scales. What they really want is an end to their own feelings of complicity. And if Indigenous peoples have to be wiped out, gradually ground into dust, for them to avoid a hard look in the mirror? So be it.

In discussing reconciliation and the history of Canada, I've been told to "get over it" too many times to count. *Get over the genocide of your ancestors. Get over the loss of your language. Get over the destruction of the environment.* It's always said as though I'm the one who's failed to properly process the events of the past, as though the crimes ended long ago and I just haven't caught up. There is, of course, an irony to being told how to interpret history by someone completely ignorant of it. It's not me who has to get over the past—I resigned myself to the facts long ago and resolved to do what needs to be done about them. It's the person hurling invective who's in real need, and what that person has to get over is fear—fear of history and fear of truth.

This is the one sense in which "reconciliation" actually describes the process Canada must undertake: non-Indigenous people must reconcile themselves to the truth of their history, the truth of their country's origins, and the truth of its continued actions. They must also reconcile themselves to the fact that as long as our existence itself poses a threat to this country, the death of Indigenous people benefits Canada.

Each loss means one less treaty rights holder, one less land protector, one less Indian standing as proof that we've been here all along, that we persist.

The system was built to support our deaths, not our lives. That's why inequality reigns to this day. That's why there were more Indigenous children in state care in 2019 than at the height of the residential schools system. That's why 102 children in care died in the last five years in Ontario alone, and it wasn't even an election issue. That's why the incarceration rates of Indigenous people remain disproportionate to our populations. It's why when ordered, repeatedly, by the courts to end discrimination against Indigenous children, the federal government has preferred to appeal rather than comply. Individual Canadians care about our lives, but the state simply does not. The cost is too high, both financially and existentially.

These truths are ugly and bleak, but there's another that gives me hope, even as it underlines the pointlessness of all the suffering colonialism has inflicted on us. It's a truth I was first able to fully grasp thanks to my daughter.

In August 2019, the last summer we'd have before COVID-19, my family travelled to Serpent River for a gathering in honour of my Auntie Mina, my grandma Norma's sister. Mina had been the youngest of her generation, and the only one spared from attending residential school. My great-grandparents, Alex and Maggie, hid her away from Indian agents. Shortly before she reached school age, they'd also removed her sister Cora from St. Joseph's. It was already too late for the rest of the kids; they had already changed from children to survivors.

The pain and trauma inflicted in those schools, and all the things they took from my family, made Serpent River a complicated place for me. It was easy to feel estranged from it, even as so much of my family remained there, even as I remained so deeply connected to it. But that was exactly the point, wasn't it? It's still the point, the point of so much of what our family, and so many other Indigenous families, are put through: to make us uncomfortable and unfamiliar on our own land, in our own nations, in our own families; to sever the connections that make us who we are so that it's easier for colonialism to extract what it wants.

My mother and my cousins have occasionally spoken to me about their own discomfort on the rez. How they, too, can feel like outsiders, despite having spent time there, despite family members being buried there. As we age together, I've often wondered if Serpent River would ever stop feeling somewhat apart from us, as though it were keeping us at a distance.

I wanted it to be different for our kids. Their first trip to Serpent River occurred when they were quite young; a large event was being held in the community centre, and we took them up to introduce them to their relatives. All the kids from the reserve were there, many of them cousins to our children. The whole group of them were running around having an absolute blast, and my kids were immediately accepted.

In the main hall, my daughter received her first eagle feather, an honour bestowed for good works. I wouldn't receive my own until several years later.

It is through my children that Serpent River began to feel closer. Their seamless integration into life there, into the community, strengthened my own ties, strengthened those of the entire family. And with each subsequent visit that feeling of connectedness has only grown. With my children leading me by the hand, Serpent River has gone from the unfamiliar to the welcoming.

On our most recent trip, Julie had to leave early to get back to work, and so I drove home alone with the kids. We went by way of Manitoulin Island, since we'd stayed a night there on the trip up and my son had left his beloved stuffed bear at the inn. As we drove down Highway 17 on our way to retrieve it, my daughter spoke up from the back seat.

"Dad?" she said.

"Yeah?"

"Can we live in Serpent River?"

"Oh no, not right now. Why? Did you have fun?"

"Yes, I love it here. I wish it could be home."

"That's wonderful. That makes me so happy," I told her. I tried to hide my tears and keep my eyes on the road. I did sneak one glance back over my shoulder and saw her staring out the window, watching the rocks and trees whizz past.

Two generations.

All the effort Canada put into forcing my family's estrangement from our land, divorcing us from our community. All that money and violence, and all it got them was two generations. My mother and me. That's it. All the work to drive my grandmother away, to brutalize her into a life in the city, and yet her great-granddaughter wants to move back to the rez. What a waste. What a colossal waste of time, money, effort, and lives. Sure, maybe you could say Canada got the land, but even that's fleeting. This country is only holding it for a while.

The same dynamic is evident throughout First Nations, Métis, and Inuit communities. Young people are re-engaging with their communities, their languages, and their land, and diving into the politics that influence them. Indigenous people are present in a wider variety of media. Our young people are on the front lines of protests. It feels as if the future is there, waiting for us to shape it. And while there is much to overcome, much to heal, and so much to change, it feels as if we're ready for that work—ready to fight.

All that effort and what did it get you, Canada: a hundred and fifty years? Maybe a little less? You threw everything you could at us, every degradation, every act of violence, every means of erasure, and we're still here. We're not going anywhere, and we'll end up getting back all that was taken.

So, just stop. Stop taking our kids, stop robbing our communities, stop jailing us, stop dehumanizing us—just stop. It didn't work. You tried everything from outright war to financial siege to pernicious attacks on family and community, and yet here's my thirteen-year-old Anishinaabe daughter, who possesses one of the most marginalized identities in the world, and all she wants is to live with her family, her people, on the same land where they've lived for millennia. Sure, she doesn't speak her language yet. She can learn. At thirteen, she already feels more at home at Cutler than I ever have.

This is how we will heal—over generations. This is how we will get back everything—over time. We were here long before you, Canada. We will be here long after.

Of course, we can get there quicker, build a new and functional relationship faster and with less pain and fear for everyone, if some things just stop. The words of politicians offer me little hope on that score—no matter how well-chosen. But I'm still optimistic.

I'm optimistic because I see in my children and in Indigenous youth across Canada just how tough and resilient we are. And I'm optimistic because more and more Canadians seem to know that great change is required.

The murder of George Floyd in May 2020 felt like a last straw. When Floyd's death was so soon followed, in Canada, by the deaths of two First Nations people during interactions with police—even as people took to the streets to protest police violence—it felt as though the world was collapsing.

Black and Indigenous people face state violence every single day— before the pandemic, during the pandemic, and, let's be realistic, after the pandemic, too. But coming during the lockdown, while Black and Indigenous people were already being more severely affected by COVID-19 than other communities, those particular acts of violence felt like salt poured in an open wound.

Maybe that's why we immediately saw public protest on an unrivalled scale, why so many were willing to risk their health and safety to take to the streets to demand change.

Or maybe it was that people who were locked down, hiding from a virus, had less to distract them and more time to listen, more time to march, more time to learn, more time to understand.

Or it was the pandemic itself, exposing as it has so much of the rot that underlies the Western capitalist system: the degradation of the environment, of people's rights and very lives in the service of shareholder gain and the sick belief that all that exploitation is somehow sustainable when all the evidence tells us it's not. The pandemic gave us the time and space to think while simultaneously delivering the same clear message: Just stop.

Stop the endless consumption. Stop the endless work to feed that consumption. Stop the hoarding—of everything, by so few. Stop the police; stop them from killing us, stop them from provoking us in order to imprison us. Stop the nationalism that blinds so many to the failure and corruption of their leaders, that sows division when we most need to rely on one another. Stop keeping people poor and sick. Just. Stop.

These systems won't work to eradicate Indigenous life and culture. We are too strong. And they won't work to keep people happy, fulfilled, and safe. They are too weak. They need to stop. Something new needs to take their place. We need change.

What I'm asking now is for all of you to help bring it about, to cast aside your fear of an unknown future and embrace this moment as an opportunity to build the country that Canada has always aspired to be—the one it pretends to be—one that recognizes the inevitable failure built into colonialism, one that recognizes Indigenous sovereignty as crucial to the realization of Canadian sovereignty. This is the Canada our ancestors envisioned when they signed the peace and friendship treaties: a collective of nations, living as they want, sharing the land mutually.

I know that vision can be realized, not because I have faith in Canada but because I believe in its people. Our systems and structures need to be dismantled and replaced, but these are problems created by humans and they can be solved by humans. In social justice movements across North America we see engaged and imaginative young people who are fighting for a truly equitable vision of society. Like them we can build new relationships and, in doing so, transform this nation into something that better reflects our values, our thoughts, ourselves.

We can't rely on governments, institutions, or companies to do this. They won't. Only we, the people, can and must solve this most human of problems.

Despite all that's been done to Indigenous peoples, despite all that continues to be done to us and will be done to us today and tomorrow, we were here before Canada and we'll be here long after it.

Show us that the myth of this country can be replaced by truth, because, frankly, we have shown you enough.

It's your turn.

Acknowledgments

I would like to thank my entire family, especially my wife, Julie, and my children for allowing me the space to write this book, and for giving me all the reason I need to live, work, and love. Thanks as well to my parents, Connie and Jim, and my sister, Maggie, for their steady encouragement. My cousins Marilyn and Steve provided valuable family history as well as lots of support. Miigwetch.

Writer Alicia Elliott was a source of great advice and inspiration. Nia:wen. Thanks to Evan Rosser for helping get my voice to the page. Thanks to Scott Sellers, Nicole Winstanley, and Diane Turbide at Penguin Random House Canada who thought this book was a good idea and helped bring it into existence. I hope you're happy now! Copyeditor Karen Alliston's skill was much appreciated. And thanks to my agent, Ron Eckel at CookeMcDermid, who helped me navigate the process.

One of the people who has always been there for me and has helped me grow and learn is Alexia McKinnon. We first met through the Banff

Centre, which has been very supportive of this book and of me. Thanks, Lexi, I hope you enjoyed reading this—you really helped make it possible!

Thanks to everyone who has listened to me on CBC radio. You are the reason why there's a book. And to all those I've worked on radio programs with, you're why people were listening in the first place.

And special thanks to the community that has picked me up when I've fallen and lifted me up when I've climbed. I hope I can do the same in return.